WICCA SPELL BOOK FOR BEGINNERS

LEARN WITCHCRAFT RITUALS, WHITE, RED, BLACK, AND RUNE MAGIC WITH THIS EASY-TO-READ GUIDE

FRANK BAWDOE

© Copyright 2021 - All rights reserved.

It is not legal to reproduce, duplicate, or transmit any part of this document in either electronic means or in printed format. Recording of this publication is strictly prohibited and any storage of this document is not allowed unless with written permission from the publisher except for the use of brief quotations in a book review.

CONTENTS

Special Bonus! v
Introduction vii

1. Witchcraft Rituals 1
2. White Magic Spells 15
3. Red Magic Spells Hoodoo 69
4. Sorcery/Hex Spells 87
5. Rune Casting & Divination 115

Final Thoughts 147
Sources 153

SPECIAL BONUS!

Thank you for adding this book to your Wiccan Library! To learn more, why not join Frank's Wiccan Community and get this additional Free Wicca Starter Kit Book 100% FREE!

Hundreds of others are already enjoying insider access to all of my current and future full-length books, 100% free!

If you want insider access plus this Free Wicca Starter Kit Book, all you have to do is scan the code below with your smartphone camera to claim your offer!

INTRODUCTION

Believe it or not, there are more than a million practicing Wiccans and pagans in the U.S. today. Wicca is a commonly misunderstood religion whose members identify themselves as "witches." It is a peaceful, spiritual and nature-based practice that has zero to do with Satanism. Nowadays, there is a growing misunderstanding that a person who identifies as being a witch is "the Wicked Witch of the West."

Frank Bawdoe is an author and devoted spiritualist who is resolved in his dedication to the philosophy of Wicca and Paganism. Frank has a deep desire to coach readers in their desire to learn about the essence of life and to teach and empower them on the basics and fundamentals of magic spells. Included in this book are the different options for crafting spells. They include multiple different types of spells, tools, materials, proper instructions, and information necessary for you to succeed with the magic spells you will practice based off of this book. Frank Bawdoe has authored numerous books on Wicca and Paganism, including *Witchcraft Religion & Spirituality and New Age Divination*. An ardent knowledge seeker who proudly walks the path leading to spirituality, he leverages his knowledge to understand the fascinating ways of life.

Exploring the depths of paganism with utmost faith and persistence for truth, Frank studies the Wiccan culture, meditation, visualization, magic, and spells to build a better connection with his inner self. Passionate about transforming lives and directing souls, Frank Bawdoe pens down his knowledge of successful spell casting and with his words and he shines a light on the path leading to self-development, happiness, and spirituality. Frank never missed out on an opportunity to embrace the beauty of life, and surrounds himself with nature that scintillates the soul and soothes the mind. He devotes his free time to reading, writing, meditating, and exploring the mysteries of life.

Learning magic spells can actually enhance your life, help you to solve challenging problems, and improve your mental ability. With this magical guide to the powerful and best witchcraft spells, you can be the captain of your own ship steering through the tides of destiny. If you're new to spell craft, you must be familiar with the usual stereotype portrayed by Hollywood. The truth is that modern day Wiccan witchcraft is a spiritual and reliable way to express your deepest intentions and then make them come true. A spell is just a ritual where you use your energy, intentions, and inner-spiritual powers to fulfill a specific purpose you desire. Protective or white magic has never really been discouraged like destructive or Black magic, for obvious reasons.

WITCHCRAFT RITUALS/SPELLS

You are conducting a ritual when you cast spells because you are creating a change in the direction you want your path or your journey in life to follow. To be successful in goal attainment, it is important to symbolize your dedication, which means focusing your energy and efforts into your intentions while performing the ritual. It is also very important to display your gratefulness to a Deity or Higher Self when you end a session, thanking them for connecting with you and changing your life for the better! Hence, you must make sure to be concise about what you *really* want. That is the only way it works. If you are not absolutely sure about exactly what you want, how would you know if your spell worked, anyway? Imagine the actual images and attach them to your words. Keep a very positive frame of mind (**knowing** that you will achieve your desires), and then, we will discuss how to have your own key for unlocking the door that leads to wherever you wish. The power of the spell will give you the willpower to keep consistency in your life.

If you are just starting out, know this: many people cast spells and perform rituals every day. You do not have to be an experienced witch to create a sacred space and cast your spells at home. You just have to know a few basics, such as the importance of positive energy that raises your vibrations; the location also has to be a calm and safe personal space to practice your magic. If you want fast results, you need to have great confidence in your spell and how you cast it. Empowerment is essential to make magic happen, and you can get that from your inner strength. Whether you are female or male, learning the techniques of witchery will enable you to master your practice and fulfill your desire to become a skilled spell caster. Rituals and spells can bring opportunities into your life, but it will still be up to you whether or not to seize those opportunities and achieve your true potential. Your patience and efforts will pay off if you believe in your spell and stay focused during the session. The two essential aspects of casting successful spells are focus and belief.

1

WITCHCRAFT RITUALS

INTENTION

AN INTENTION IS MAKING A DECISION ABOUT WHAT YOU WANT TO achieve with a spell, and then, communicating it as concisely and specifically as you possibly can. Part of the reason you are setting an intention is to clearly communicate your desires. It is important to let the deities (or the universe or higher power) know exactly what you want. Remember you are co-creating magic with a power other than yourself. Another important purpose for your intention is to not manifest the wrong outcome by mistake.

Let's say you want more money so you cast a money spell, but it is really because you hate your job. The question here is murky. Set your truths in your intention. It may not be more money that you actually want. Maybe it is life satisfaction! Maybe the spell you need to do is for finding work that you love that will also bring financial abundance.

Another purpose of your intention is where the power in the spell comes from. Once you have set your intention, you can support it with your feelings and thoughts and when put together, it will harness the power you need to make it happen. That is how to create the strongest possible intention! As you become a more powerful witch, you will see more positive changes happening in your life. New opportunities will open up for you. When you feel a deep connection to your own intuition and to the powers that be, you will start to have the confidence to take even bigger risks for bigger payoffs and make leaps and bounds towards your goals. You can get excited as a newbie witch to see for yourself that magic is real! Here is a word of caution: if a spell doesn't work the first time, don't let that stop you from trying your hand at spell casting again and again. You will soon learn there are some other factors that go into successful spellcasting.

Setting a strong and clear intention prior to beginning is the best way to power up your spell. Afterall, it is the intention of the witch that makes or breaks the spell! Here is a simple formula for the beginner or intermediate witch to try:

1. **A specific want (as precise as you can) + the time frame you want it to manifest = your intention**.
2. Write your intention down using "I" and a verb in the present tense, as if it has already been manifested. For example: "I run two miles a week to better my health" feels stronger than "Help me to make it two miles when I run."
3. Test your intention. Once you have written down an accurate and clear intention, conduct the following ritual(s) to test it.
4. Journal Ritual: In a safe and calm atmosphere where you know there will be no distractions for at least ten minutes, scribe a candle and get comfortable. (You will also learn how to create a sacred space). Start journaling about how your life is at the present. Be as specific as you feel comfortable with. If you are doing a

spell for love, journal your current relationship status. Write about its ups and downs. If you are looking for love, journal about what your life will feel like after you find your soulmate. What you will do together. How it feels to go for a walk on the beach with that special someone.

5. Once you feel you have filled in all of the specifics, you can write your actual intention. For example, a good intention may be written something like this: "This month, I meet a special person who I have a spiritual, emotional, and physical connection with. We love each other passionately and openly and we are both so happy that we are going to travel together."
6. Spiritual Connection Ritual Meditation
7. Sit calmly and quietly with your eyes closed.
8. Make a decision with whom you are communicating:
9. The Triple Goddess
10. The Great Horned God
11. The Green Man
12. Goddess Brighid
13. The horned fertility god Cernunnos
14. Isis
15. The Elements (Air, Fire, Earth, Water, Spirit)
16. Your intuition
17. Aloud, ask your spiritual guide "What is my desire?"
18. Now listen. Pay close attention to any smells, sights, sounds, and tastes; notice your thoughts as they glide through your mind as you rest there. That could be your spirit communicating with you.
19. If you are not receiving an answer, ask again. Ask as often as you have to until you feel you have completed your intention.
20. Visualize your Intention
21. With your eyes closed for a specific amount of time, in your mind's eye, picture your life after your desire has

been met. Focus on a specific scene; a moment in time that you believe totally represents what your life will be like after your spell. For example: If you desire a new love interest, you can picture a scene with a new love in your mind of the two of you cuddled up on the couch, popcorn in the middle, watching *Gone with the Wind*. You will notice fairly fast if you have the right intention because you will already be viewing the results in your mind's eye, just like watching a movie! If something is not quite right, make some adjustments here and there in your scene and try again. Tweak it as much as you have to until your intention is exactly what you want.

CLEARING AND CLEANSING RITUAL

Clearing and cleansing your space and yourself is like making a blank energetic slate. Smudging is always the first line of defense to rid or ward off unwanted or negative energy. Using plants, like sage and resins to rid unwanted and negative energy, will strengthen your intention and put you in the right mindset for magic! Sage actually has antibacterial properties.

First off, making your area sacred requires clearing all of the noise and clutter so that the elements and the spirit world can hear you clearly.

1. With a vacuum and dust rag, get rid of all dirt and dust from your sacred space. If you are in your office, have an organized desk.
2. Take a ritual shower. It shows respect for the magic. Hang a bit of eucalyptus in the shower for its healing properties.
3. Feel free to adorn your workplace with crystals to enhance your spell work. Choose them according to the spell.

4. Optionally, spray any counter tops or furniture with witch hazel.
5. Run a selenite wand over your body from the bottom of your feet to the top of your head, covering all of your chakras while focusing your intention on riding the area of negativity.
6. Use sound bowls and tuning forks. They help vibrate energy right into your body and your spirit.
7. Smudge: smudging frees the spirit of protection in the plant to help you with your magic. Make sure to show great appreciation for the resin or plant you burn! If you have a bundle, simply light one end on fire and then blow it out. Wave the smoke over all of your chakras, reaching down to the floor, up in front of you, and behind you (if you are limber enough to do so, if not, there is a healing spell for that too). If you are using loose tea or herbs, keep them in a fireproof container, light them up, and when they smoke, using a feather or your hand, wave the smoke over your body. Smudge everything you want cleansed, including your tools, altar, even the whole room. Pay special attention to doorways and corners.
8. If you can't handle smoke or you want to smudge a space where smoke is not allowed, buy a smudging spray from a trusted metaphysical store online, or make a cleaning spray.
9. Smokeless Smudging Recipe: 1 oz. Clean spray bottle, six drops of sage essential oil, 1 tablespoon witch hazel, 1 teaspoon sea salt, spring water or water blessed by the moon, and a small clear quartz crystal that will fit into the bottle. Combine all ingredients and spray your area.

CANDLE MAGIC

In case you are wondering if you have yet to perform magic, ask yourself if you have ever made a wish before you blew out the candles on your birthday cake. Effective, easy, and quick, practicing candle magic doesn't require any experience or a religious doctrine. Candles are a great place to start your magic practice. They are easy to collect and most are inexpensive and beautiful to have around your home. There is just something so special about the glow of a candle. It is mesmerizing. Are you ready to create some wonderful candle magic? Let's start!

Step One:

Your magic wand is your words; speak your intention. Take some deep breaths to clear your mind. Ask yourself what you wish to manifest right now in your life and tell yourself that you are planting your wish into the universe like planting a seed in the soil. It is very important to understand that there is no such thing as putting a spell on someone. Instead of wishing for Michael at the gym to notice you finally, wish for your own special and beautiful mojo to be enhanced to bring you the very best love interest in your life. Using positive energy, create your intention into a condensed powerful and clear sentence.

Step Two:

Decide if your intention is big or small. For a quick lift, you can grab some of those small white candles at the local grocery store and they only take about two hours to burn down. If you're asking for something a bit bigger and want to concentrate your positive vibrations on it for a week or two, you can use a glass seven-day candle to do the trick. The size or your candle doesn't matter nearly as much as how much intention, focus, and energy you put into it. You can make a more powerful ritual candle through anointing, carving, and/or dressing it. You can dress your candle in oils and herbs, such as rose oil or olive oil. You also can blend oils to match your intentions such as money oils or love oils. To conjure up a vial of money oil start with ⅛ cup extra virgin olive oil, and then put 2 drops each of ginger and vetiver, 1 drop of orange, and 5 drops each of sandalwood and patchouli. You can find recipes for oils online.

Next, think about carving your intention into your candle. Outline any symbols or just write in words your intention starting at the top of the candle, then carve into the middle and the bottom. Rub your hands in your anointing oil and rub down your candle as if you are manifesting your intentions into the candle starting at the top, all the way down to the bottom. However, if you are doing a banishing ritual, start rubbing your oil in the middle first, rub toward the top, then back to the middle, then to the bottom. Follow the same ritual with herbs, sprinkling them in the same patterns. Also, you can take different color candle wax and drip it on top of your oil or herbs to keep your herbs fixed on the candle. Only use a small bit of herbs; you don't want them to catch fire.

Step Three:

Magic with colors can express many different emotions which are unique to each one of us. Think about the color of your intention.

A guideline is included below:

Color	Intention	Magic Tips
Red	Love, passion	Wear a sexy red scarf or article of clothing when you lit your red candle for added intent.
Orange	Confidence, creativity	Mindfully, with intention, peel and eat an orange each day from a bowl of oranges kept on your kitchen or dining table. Then lit your orange candle and you will have added intent.
Pink	Friendship, self-care, empathy, nurturance	Carve your name into your pink candle to show self-love before lighting it. Or carve a friend's name you mean good for.
Purple	Empowerment, royalty	Add some lavender oil or spray in the room where you are lighting the candle. Dance around your candle in the lavender scent before or after lighting.
Blue	Calm, peace, protection	Keep some seashells by your candle or in a bowl of water.
Green	Money, starting a new business, fertility	Light your candle while sitting outside, if not too windy, or wear green nail polish or a green shirt.
White	Blank slate, add sprinkles to make it the color you need. White fills in for all colors	Meditate while imagining a white orb surrounding your body after lighting your candle.

Step Four:

Write or type down your daily vision, the color of your candle. Scripting on to your candle will give your vibration an instant boost. Scripting is about writing down your calling for the day as if you have already achieved it. Write down the details, describing to yourself how it feels and what your sensations of happiness, joyousness, and freedom feel like. This will elevate your energy vibrations. Now, you are ready to carve your candle. If you do not want to burn the entire candle, carve a line however far down you want to burn to confine your spell into the top section. When it burns down to that line you can blow it out and save the rest of the candle for another spell.

OPENING AND CLOSING A CIRCLE RITUAL

> *"We are a circle, within a circle, with no beginning and never ending."*

While facing north, speak aloud "I am grateful for your energy, precious earth; farewell." Closing or opening a circle is a technique for respecting the elements and thanking them for assisting you to take all of the energy you have built and release it. Next, while facing west, you will release the water and speak aloud "I am grateful for your energy, precious Water; I bid you adieu." Do the same with fire while facing south "Farewell Fire, thank you for your energy." End on the north, releasing the element spirit, "Spirit, I bid you goodbye for now, I close this circle, sending the energy back into the ground".

Step-by-Step Instruction on How to Cast a Circle

1. Scrub your space with burning sage, vacuum and clean it.
2. Mark the directions and elements with crystals or candles. Using a cross pattern set the south, north, east and west. Use a pentacle if you're also including the spirit.
3. Face east and name each element, moving clockwise to each point. "I call upon the element of fire." "I call upon you, Earth."
4. Meditate for a few minutes until you feel centered and grounded.
5. Connect with each element, envisioning in your mind how the wind feels blowing around you, how the water

feels, etc., until you have called and connected to each element and completed your circle.
6. Now you should be facing north; imagine yourself shooting light from the bottom of your feet down into the Earth's core and pulling back its energy. State aloud "With these five elements and under the Spirit of the Goddess, I cast protection above, below, and within this circle!"
7. You are now ready to cast your spells.

CREATING YOUR ALTAR

You can cast spells without being at your altar, of course, but having one is a very good place to practice and focus your intention and energy. It is a sacred space where you can communicate with the elements, goddesses, and the spirit realm in general. It doesn't have to be a special table; you can make one just about anywhere you feel drawn to. I have mine in my office, in the corner facing the west to see the sunset. I have had many altars, but a while back, I decided I wanted an altar that I could leave spell work upon without disturbance. A spell works for as long as you have it placed, in writing or words, along with all of the magical items supporting it on the altar. Every Wiccan's or pagan's journey is unique to them, so make sure you feel connected to anything that touches your altar.

Choose a cloth that you love for your altar. You can choose any pattern, color, or texture. I strongly suggest using something natural. You can even use a bamboo matt or silk; it really is up to your intuition.

Here are some helpful hints for picking the color of your cloth:

Red	Fire	Love, physical energy, desire passion, will power, courage
Green	Earth	Abundance, money, fertility, nature, health, luck
Yellow	Air	Intelligence, happiness, memory
Blue	Water	Wisdom, spirituality, calmness
Orange	Fire	Buying property, intellect, justice
Pink	Fire	Friendship, nurturing, healing, romance
Brown	Earth	Nature, family, animals, gardening, cooking, grounding
White	Air	Cleansing, purity, peace, light, inspiration, clarity
Purple	Spirit	Acceptance, sexuality, balance, psychic attributes
Silver	Water	Astral projection, dreams, telepathy, intuition
Gold	Fire	Fame, fortune, wealth, luck, attention enlightenment,

If honoring a deity, include symbols or items that are attributed to them and their magic. Use your intuition when and where you are placing sacred items on your altar. Usually, five candles are placed on the altar in the four corners and in the middle. Also, you can place items representing the earth, water, fire and air. I use a glass bowl filled with purified water, small candles floating atop, and a small opal crystal at the bottom. I am exalting honor to water on the altar's west side. You can use any type of items symbolizing what you want, but here are some suggestions:

- East (Air) — Wing, feather, knife, magnifying glass, wind chimes, incense;
- West (Water) — Driftwood, seaweed, goblet, river rocks, water bowl, seashells, salt, crystal ball;
- South (Fire) — Cactus, candles, lava stones. yellow flowers, orange or red crystals, matches, spicy foods;
- North (Earth) — bones, plants, rocks, small trees, seeds, soil.

RUNES RITUAL

Usually inscribed in stone, the runic alphabet contains symbols that, when read, will give you answers and great insight regarding any situations or questions you may ask them. There are 24 runes, the first six of which spell the word *futhark*. The term rune means "hidden secret" or "mystery." The word *futhark* is the name of the writing system used as early as the 3rd century by Germanic people, mainly Anglo-Saxons and Scandinavians. With runes, you can use your magic to seek advice and give yourself insight into your future or someone else's. Practicing fortune-telling techniques is knowing the art of runic divination.

How to read runes:

1. Meditate in a quiet place focusing on the story you want to read. Put some deep thought into the questions.
2. Call upon the elements, goddess, or spirit of your choice to guide you.
3. Choose one rune and think about why it is significant. After some practice you can work on layouts and casts.
4. The Three Rune Layout: randomly pick and place three runes on your sacred cloth. Place the first rune to the right, the second one in the middle, and the third one to the left. The last one is your question or the past. The middle one is the present or the present challenge. The first one rune is the answer or the future.
5. The Five Rune Layout: pick five runes and place face up or face down in the following pattern: #1-middle, #2 to its left; #3 -top: #4-bottom; #5-right place the rest in pattern of a cross encircling #1 around it. 2-5-1 horizontally symbolize your past, present and future. #4 identifies the problem or challenge you are asking

or facing. and #3 gives you what you are seeking (truth-answers).

6. The Nine Rune Cast: select 9 runes and cup them in your hands for a couple of minutes while meditating on your quest. Scatter them randomly. The middle rune is the current situation or your question. The outer edges of the scatter are less relevant. Notice if the runes are touching; they may be associated. Those that have fallen opposite each other symbolize opposing forces, actions, ideas, or thoughts. Runes that fell face up are for reflection and those that are upside down are the future.

2

WHITE MAGIC SPELLS

Casting a spell happens when you focus your intentions on your desired outcome and then stay positive about it to manifest your desired outcome. It takes a lot of practice, so be okay with losing your focus here and there. It happens to me a lot. I find meditation really helps me to not lose my focus during spell work. First, here is a simple recipe that you will probably use more than you realize. It is a moon-blessing spell.

CRYSTAL MAGIC

Crystals and other mineral stones are surprisingly versatile and are powerful agents of magic. Witches and other pagans use crystals for many positive intentions, such as prosperity, love, health and wellness, and for cleansing and charging other magical tools. If you have ever looked closely at a gemstone while holding it up to the light, you can see the wonder of these special rocks and can be easily overcome with a sense of awe. The term crystal is defined as any material naturally formed by a geological process inside the Earth. Each crystal has its own special vibrational energy; the most popular is clear quartz. You will notice many of the spells in the book use crystals as a powerful vehicle for carrying your intentions and your intuition in your craft.

Many witches consider crystals to be living organisms because of the healing energies they provide. Many give off electrical charges you can see if you simply tap them with a small hammer. Spell casters understand that crystal magic is the same as magic produced by the elements as they occur naturally, like powerful storms and rushing rivers. All energies, both visible and invisible are interconnected. Since our thoughts and our intentions are also energy forms, crystals work as conduits, sending our desires and powers out into the spiritual world.

ESSENTIAL OILS AND MAGIC

Using essential oils in magic is not a new trend by any means. Ancient Egyptians used essential oils for religious ceremonies thousands of years ago. Currently, most people have experienced aromatherapy. They either love using it in their homes or when getting a massage. Essential oils affect people on many levels. Smelling an essential oil for its calming effects or to stimulate creativity are two common "everyday" ways people practice magic, whether they know it or not. Less conventionally, essential oils are used in our magic rituals. Most experienced witches are familiar with the magical properties contained in essential oils, but if you are new to the practice, know now they are very powerful tools for every witch's tool kit.

Considering the fact that this is a book of spells, it is quite obvious that many ingredients or materials go into the art of magic. Ginger, sage, sugar, salt, garlic, basil, are just a few of the common ingredients. Essential oils are used to amplify the magic of these ingredients. They are used to charge crystals, in rituals, talisman, amulets, and even to anoint our physical bodies. In addition, they are also used to create powerful witchcraft goods. Candles, charms, and incense are often enhanced with a drop or two of an essential oil tailored to their intention. Essential oils are extracted from the stems, leaves, and flowers of varying types of plants. Plants carry magical energies as they are intelligent living beings. That alone makes them powerfully magical. Each plant has its own unique magical properties, and when concentrated in an oil, its magical abilities are amplified. It is important that you know to only use natural oils. Synthetic oils may smell good; however, they are not natural and are not the same as the derivatives found in botanical oils. Also, the powerful scent of an essential oil has a profound impact on the spirit, mind, and body. Hence, they are capable of altering the way the mind thinks. Just think about how you feel about your favorite scent. Does it make you happy, elevate your mood, ease your stress, or make you feel dreamy? Now, that is magic!

TYPES OF MAGICAL ESSENTIAL OILS

1. Lemon: regarded highly for its magic in promoting clarity. Also increases your energy levels, enhances your overall wellbeing, and has rejuvenating properties.
2. Lavender: regarded highly for its relaxation and anxiety reducing properties. It is a mood stabilizer and can be used in love spells, healing spells, sleep spells, dream recall spells, healing spells, and more.
3. Eucalyptus: is known to improve your ability to concentrate. It is also a purifying agent, dream stimulator, and can be used for many issues surrounding the nose, throat, lungs, and muscular issues.
4. Peppermint: is amazing at promoting mental clarity. It

also provides protection, invites love, stimulates regeneration, and is an antiseptic used for purification and cleansing.
5. Chamomile: prized for its extreme anti-anxiety qualities and used to alleviate insomnia. This essential oil will elevate your inner peace, calm your anger, and heighten sexual arousal. It is also used for good luck and elevated spiritual awareness. Chamomile is a powerful meditation agent.
6. Clove: is used to boost energy levels, ward off the evil eye, purifying, ritual cleansing, and pain management. It has highly invigorating qualities and sparks nostalgia.
7. Frankincense: is a very ancient essential oil that provides great comfort, evokes visions, improves concentration, and is regarded highly in purification rituals.
8. Jasmine: known as the love drawing essential oil, jasmine also attracts love on a spiritual level, so it is the essential oil of choice for anyone searching for their soulmate.
9. Cinnamon: if you want to protect your home from all that is negative, use cinnamon essential oil in your protection spells. As it is an oil connected to the Fire Element, it is very good for stimulating the libido. It is also used in money drawing spells and will give any of your intentions a hefty boost.

ESSENTIAL HERBS AND MAGIC

Historically, there was no difference between medicine and magic. Without the rich tradition of European magic, science, and pharmacology, present-day medicines and science would never have come to be. There is a plethora of supportive documentation as to the essential role of herbal magic in the origin of present-day medicine. The only way to truly comprehend the role herbal magic plays in modern medicine is to know how it started and what it has come to be throughout the past millennium. Natural magic, as it was referred to at the start of the 1900s, was predominantly anchored in the assumption that the world was created by God in a continuous chain of life, where every element was not only linked but corresponded to another element in the unbroken chain created by God and underlying it all is purpose. Since God doesn't make any mistakes, there is a purpose for all that exists in the universe. It was understood that clues were left by the Creator or God (e.g., the flesh of a walnut in its shell and the human brain) and that magic was part of how we can affect one another. The role of the magician was to discover these correspondences and their specific magical effect and use it for the purpose of humankind.

Herbal healing, like other forms of magic, dates back to the beginning of humankind. The history of this relationship is documented by original plant medicines and herbs themselves becoming preserved historical monuments. Acknowledgment of the herbal use in pharmacology started with the pursuit of medicine through using flowers, barks, leaves, stems, seeds, and fruits of plants to remedy illness and disease. Modern day medicine has realized that the active ingredients in herbs contribute to a wide range of medicines which originate in plants. This was known to ancient civilizations and has been used throughout millennia.

MAGICAL HERBS

1. Sage: is familiar to most witches, having been used in smudging rituals to expel negative energy left behind by repulsive furniture or even more revolting exes. For

rituals, make sure to use natural sage or garden sage. White sage has become at-risk for being over-harvested so growing a bit of your own is helpful or substitute it with any form of culinary sage.

2. Rosemary: is used for many purposes. It has a stimulating scent and helps with memory. It has attributes in the areas of healing, love, protection, and feminine powers. You can hang it in your doorway, sprinkle it on the floor prior to a sweep, or in an essential oil to anoint your body.

3. Roses: are for love and friendship and so much more. Roses in the herbal world are known for calming the nervous system and unblocking and balancing the heart chakra. Fresh petals can be used for a love bath, infused into blessed water, and placed on your altar for self-care rituals.

4. Basil: is distinctly pronounced as a magical herb, making it a staple in the gardens of many a witch. It has a reputation that is sacred, dating back to ancient cultures. It keeps you focused, brings a business good luck, repels unwanted love interests, mends rifts that occur in friendships, and protects your house and your sacred circles.

5. Mint: raises the vibrations of a sacred circle, altar, and bedroom. It is used to attract positive spirits, love, to stimulate sexual arousal, attract visions, and to attract money. It has various medicinal properties as well as being a digestive aid and soothing agent for sore throats and colds. Mint is also connected to Hades because it was used to cover the scent expelled from dead bodies during funeral ceremonies in ancient Greece.

6. Mugwort: enhances psychic dreaming and divination. Its magical uses include working against fatigue, poisons, and injury. It is thought to induce astral

traveling and lucid dreaming. It can be smoked, consumed as a spice, or applied to the skin. It can be used for many psychic teas and divinatory incenses.

7. Vervain: is used for protection, purification, consecrating and cleansing sacred spaces, and in ritual magic. When consumed as a tea, it helps in divination and astral projection. It is the herb of love potions and love spells.

8. Lavender: wards off evil eye and promotes peace. It is used for calming and purification. It has been documented as far back as before the time of Christ to relieve sore throats, headaches, and indigestion. Modern magic uses lavender for stress management, anxiety, digestion, fatigue, and more. It can be burned and the ashes scattered to bring harmony and peace to the home and to cleanse a sacred space. When placed under a person's pillow or consumed as a tea, its healing for ailments such depression and insomnia is unrivaled. Hanging dried lavender in front of the house will drive away evil spirits.

9. Cinnamon: is used to purify the home or sacred space of negative energy. It can be steeped into an elixir for heightened clairvoyance and psychic abilities. It is used to draw money and is great to keep in a mojo bag for inspiration. Hang a bundle over your front door to protect against outsiders with bad intentions; or make it part of your love spells. Bake a custard or cake for blessings of everlasting love and serve it in a meal if you want some luck for the night. Put it in your bag of runes for added clairvoyant energy.

FRANK'S "MOON-BLESSED WATER" RECIPE

Ingredients:

- 1 Moonstone or clear quartz crystal
- A full moon
- 1 Stick cinnamon
- 1 lavender colored flower
- Glass jar or bottle with cork
- Cauldron or cast-iron pot for boiling
- Cheesecloth, coffee filter, or strainer
- Funnel
- 1 White floating candle

What to do:

1. Find out when the next full moon occurs, you're going to need it.
2. Gather all of your ingredients on the full moon night. If you are feeling super witchy, do this spell with a traditional pot on the flames of your bonfire! Or just use a stovetop burner.
3. Bring the herbs and water to a boil. If you put them in a cheesecloth or wrap and tie them in a coffee filter, you won't have to strain the liquid later.
4. Let the whole kit and kaboodle simmer on a low heat for 30 minutes.
5. After it cools, strain the herbs into the glass bowl.
6. At midnight, go with your bowl outside and put it where you can see the moon's reflection in the water.
7. Place your clear quartz or moonstone crystal in the middle of the bowl.
8. Light your candle and send it floating in your moonlit water. You can either meditate until it burns out or ask

the Goddesses to compliment the moon with her blessings. Leave it there until the next day.
9. The next day, pick out the cold wax from the candle encasement.
10. Pour the water through the funnel.
11. Thank all spirits involved and your materials.
12. Keep it handy!

FRANK'S HEALING SPELL TO KEEP YOU SAFE AND SOUND (BASIC HEALING SPELL)

Materials

- Candles
- 1 White for cleansing, peace, and purity
- 1 Pink for close friendships
- 1 Green for health and prosperity
- 1 Purple for spiritual strength
- Crystal: 1 Clear Quartz (master healer)
- Pen and paper to scribe your name or another person or a photo of yourself or the person you want to heal. Do this spell for one person at a time for the most strength.
- Healing oils:
- Lavender is a natural antidepressant, decongestant, good for skin problems, and is a natural diuretic.
- Chamomile is a natural antidepressant, antibiotic, lessens acne, anti-inflammatory and helps with insomnia. Sparks sweet dreams.
- Eucalyptus calls on the spirit of the koala bear. Promotes positivity and healing energy.
- Cinnamon oil boosts your spell's power and aids in healing and balancing chakras.
- Large plate
- Fire in the form of a lighter

Steps

1. Decide where you are going to cast your spell and cleanse your sacred area and yourself.
2. Sit down in a quiet spot with all of your ingredients in front of you.
3. Write your name or the name of the person you want to heal on a piece of paper or use a photo and put it into your fireproof container, cauldron, plate, etc.
4. Cup the clear quartz crystal in your hands to warm it up. Focus on the crystal, imagining you are filling it with love and healing energy, and then, place your crystal on top of the name or photo.
5. Fix the candle by placing one drop of each oil on each candle (anointment ritual).
6. Anoint each of your candles with a drop of each oil. All of the oils in this spell are for healing. You can use your intuition on which oil goes on each candle.
7. Place the candles in a circle around the container with the name or photo. They should be evenly spaced in the four cardinal points.
8. Using the lighter or a match, light your candles.
9. Gaze into the flames and picture a fire circling around the name or photo of yourself or the person you want to heal. Imagine the fire turning the dark to light, the suffering to healing.
10. With your eyes closed, imagine the healing glow flowing into the person through the crystal. Know they are healthy and well, vital, and glowing with energy and wellness. Speak aloud as if the healing has already taken place. "I am happy and healthy and healed. My heart is strong and healthy."
11. Picture a smile on the face of the person looking back at you with love and strength. If you are casting the spell on you, imagine how happy you are to be feeling

better, how your arms and legs feel light, and how endlessly capable you are of magic.
12. Now direct your power to the specific ailment. Imagine flooding that area with healing light; the longer and more focused you are the more powerful the spell.
13. When you feel your spell is complete. Slowly open your eyes and speak aloud

> ***With all of the magic in this spell, I cast healing energy, protection, and light to (the name of the person). I send this magic and vigor flowing through my/their being so it may heal them of their suffering. So Mote it Be.***

"PEACEFUL MIND" SPELL (FOR CALMING)

- 1 Blue candle
- 1 Purple Candle
- 1 White Candle
- A palo santo stick and fireproof dish
- White paper and a blue pen

Steps

1. Put the candles in a triangle.
2. White at the top point, blue to the right, and purple to the left.
3. Light them in this order: Blue, Purple, White.
4. Light the palo santo.
5. Speak this spell three times.

> ***I have the courage to break free and the insight to know. With the breath of this sacred smoke, calmness will grow. So Mote it be.***

1. Take ten deep breaths through your nose and out of your mouth.
2. Smudge the pen and paper with your palo santo bundle.
3. Trust in your intuition and write your intention on the paper.
4. Read what you have written and meditate on it for five minutes.
5. Keep the paper with you for as long as you need it.

BATHING SPELLS FOR SPIRITUAL CLEANSING AND PROTECTION

Spiritual bathing offers added protection, especially if you are feeling vulnerable. The following spells are ideal for strengthening your spiritual protection barriers. Spiritual bathing practices are utilized in many cultures for clearing the mind, cleansing the soul, and healing your chakras. Make sure your tub or shower is free of clutter and spotless. The ingredients mentioned below, meditation, and most of all intention, are elements for successful magic. Also, please be sure to be unplugged (no cell phone or other devices). It is time for you to meditate and focus on invoking the spirit of elements and deities for healing, protection, prosperity, and love. These spells can also be used with the intent of cleaning away negativity or unwanted situations that may be holding you back. There is no set way to take a spiritual bath. Each bath is prepared and set to each individual's needs, but if you find yourself needing assistance, below you will find some steps that others have taken to create a great spiritual bath experience.

Materials (these can be added or switched with any of the ingredients listed for bathing spells).

- Salt (The most powerful salt is black)
- Dead sea salt
- Kosher salt
- Eucalyptus oil
- Cedar oil
- Four small blue candles
- Mint leaves
- Rosemary
- Lavender

Steps

1. Protective Bath Spells
2. Protective bathing spell 1. Charge your kosher salt: "I summon the spirit of the salt to help me to protect my home and heart." Mix 5 drops of eucalyptus oil and 5 drops cedar oil with ½ cup of kosher salt with bath water.
3. Protective bathing spell 2. Basil, rosemary, lavender, mint, handful of sea salt. Run a warm bath and toss in ingredients. Save a cup of the water after bathing and toss it outside.
4. Protective bathing spell 3. Ingredients: 1 bay leaf, 1 teaspoon ground mint leaf, 1 teaspoon fresh or ground rosemary, ¼ cup coarse salt, 1 small white candle and a pot or tea kettle. If using fresh herbs, you can double the amount.
5. Add herbs to a pot of spring water and bring to a boil. Let simmer for 15 minutes.
6. While the tea is cooking, take a normal shower to physically clean yourself.
7. Light your candle and fill your tub with warm water.

8. When your tea is ready, remove herbs with a filter.
9. Starting with your head, scoop a cup of water out of the pot and pour over your spiritual bath. Work your way down to your feet.
10. While you are letting the spirit of the water flow over your body, Notice the smell, and thank Mother Earth for creating it.
11. Clear your mind during this calming time you have created for yourself.
12. Step out and pat yourself or let yourself air dry.

"MUCH-NEEDED SLEEP" SPELL

We now have a good understanding about intention being at the heart of magical practice. I can't think of a more intense intention than for someone to sleep. It is very important to combine self-care with most spells, but especially this one. Learning some deep breathing techniques, watching your caffeine intake, practicing relaxation techniques, and ritual bathing can fight insomnia. After doing all these, a bit of magic at bedtime should seal the deal. After participating in the preparation for bed techniques just outlined, you will be ready to cast the Much-Needed Sleep Spell. Smoky quartz is a powerful grounding stone and prevents nightmares and clear quartz amplifies the powers of all other crystals.

Materials

- 8 Dried lavender stems
- 1 Clear Quartz Crystal
- 1 Piece of preferably raw paper (unbleached)
- 1 Smoky Quartz Crystal

Steps

1. After you perform your ritual bathing preparation for your Much Need Sleep spell, get your bedtime area to be as comfortable as possible. Dim the lights, light a nighttime candle, use fresh bed clothes (never underestimate how freshly cleaned sheets can affect the quality and quantity of sleep), take a before bedtime trip to the restroom, making sure all of the doors are locked, the pets tended to, I think you get the point. Simply put, get ready for bed.
2. Sit comfortably in your bed. Don't sit on the pillow you use for your head. If you need an extra pillow, grab one from the couch or spare bedroom.
3. Have all of your materials within reach.
4. Hold a crystal in each hand and sync your intention with each of the crystal's energies. Notice how they feel in your hand.
5. Close your eyes and roll the crystals around in your hand, feeling every bump, curve, and shape as they slowly start to warm up with your touch.
6. Let the vibrational energies of each stone enter through your fingers, spread through your arms and down your shoulders, like a gentle wave washing over your whole body.
7. Focus on the smoky quartz crystal and realize its grounding and calming powers transforming all things negative or stressful into peace and serenity as you move its energy though your legs and down to your toes.
8. Now focus on your clear quartz and realize that suddenly hope and good thoughts are beginning to radiate from the palm of your hand.
9. Feel the energy of the magnificent clear quartz flowing through your mind, body, and soul.
10. Slip into the protective and calming energy powers of the stones while allowing your mind to quiet.

11. After a few moments with the crystals, softly speak:

> *Peaceful rest come visit me.*
> *My mind with my spirit will be free.*
> *Grant me contentment of mind tonight,*
> *so my morning will be a beautiful sight.*
> *So mote it be.*

1. Slowly open your eyes, while staying relaxed and continuing to let the calming effects of your ritual course through your body.
2. Take the rest of the ingredients (lavender sprigs and crystals) and fold them up in the piece paper like a small parcel and place them next to your bed.
3. Gently ease yourself down into your bed.
4. Thank your crystals, your lavender sprigs, and any elements or deities that accompanied you during your spell and let yourself drift off.

BLACK SALT RECIPE

Black salt or Witch's salt is used for many purposes. If you do use it for a voodoo or hexing make sure you dispose of it by burying it far from your home. Otherwise, sprinkle around the perimeter of your property, car, or anything else you want protected. It is an excellent way to cleanse and charge your crystals. You can use it to drive away bad spirits and you can sprinkle it on the footprints of anyone toxic in your life that needs to be somewhere else, anywhere else, except with you!

Ingredients

- 2 parts sea salt
- Ash from your fire pit or black pepper
- Food-grade activated charcoal (you can use dry,

powdered black food coloring but it is not as useful as ash and charcoal.)
- Grind it up with a mortar and pestle.
- Store it in a spell bowl with a small spoon that you have smudged.

"PROTECT YOUR HOME" SPELL

Steps

1. Using black salt, create a circle around you.
2. Place your 4 blue candles inside of the circle in the cardinal points.
3. Light the candles.
4. Chant:

> **"Salt of Earth Guard my home. Place it in a protective zone. Protect it from all that's dark. Hold it safely in your heart."**

1. Focus your intention as you watch in wonderment at how the flames dance for protection.
2. When you feel the spell is complete, blow out the candles.
3. Thank the spirits with your deepest gratitude for protecting your home.

HOME PROTECTION CRYSTAL ENCHANTMENT SPELL

Materials

- One small bowl
- 1 black candle
- 1 Rose quartz

- 1 Fluorite
- 1 Clear quartz
- 1 bulb of garlic
- 3 iron nails (large)
- 9-inch-long pieces of white thread (#9)
- 9-inch-long pieces of black and red thread (#6 of each)
- Water
- Wine
- 1 White Egg

Steps

1. Take 3 white pieces of thread, 2 red pieces of thread, and 2 black pieces of thread and braid them together.
2. Light the black candle
3. Let some of the wax puddle at the top of the candle and then coat the braided thread with it. This will form a magically charged wick.
4. Do the same in the same order with the rest of your thread (twice) so that you end up with 3 braided wicks.
5. Peel some of the garlic skin and enwrap one of the iron nails.
6. Wrap one of the wicks around the nail encased in garlic skin.
7. Do the same with the other two nails and two braids, so you end up with 3 braided wicks.
8. Place the 3 nails in the bowl in the shape of a triangle.
9. In the center of the triangle, place the egg.
10. Place the crystals at each point of the triangle.
11. Sprinkle it with the wine and the water.
12. Do this for 3 days.
13. On day 4, throw the egg out into your yard, bury the crystals, and drive the nails into the ground
14. So mote be (

This is a very strong spell from *The Gardnerian Book of Shadows* and should protect your house indefinitely.

"CHILDREN NEED PROTECTION" SPELL

All children including witches need protection. As adults, it is our number one priority. Their spiritual, emotional, and physical health needs to be guarded against any foul doings. This is sympathetic magic to protect a child or children whom you care for.

Materials

- 2 Small Rose Quartz Crystals
- Echinacea
- Elderberry
- White cotton
- Bright yellow cloth approximately 1 ft
- Fingernail or toenail clippings from the child
- A lock of the child's hair or children's hair
- If possible, a baby tooth
- Pen and yellow paper
- Rose essential oil
- Aquamarine Crystal
- 2 Cups of Caraway Seeds
- Yellow thread
- Super glue

Steps

1. Lay your yellow cloth our and hand draw a bear or doll (see diagram above)
2. You can draw the protection sigil on the front. It is your puppet to put your intention into.

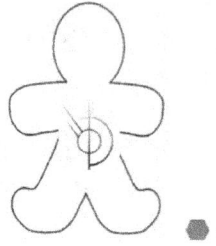

3. Cut two identical pieces.
4. Write the name of the child or children on the piece of paper.
5. Put two drops of rose essential oil on the Aquamarine crystal.
6. Using the yellow thread, sew the back to the front but leave the top open so you can stuff it later.
7. Write the child's name on the piece of paper and fold it up.
8. Put all of the child's personal items into the doll.
9. Put ½ of the seeds in the doll.
10. ½ way to the top put the child's name folded in the middle.
11. Put the other ½ caraway seeds.
12. Stuff the rest up into the top and wherever else needs it
13. Sew the top of the doll.
14. Super glue the blue crystals for eyes. If you don't want to use superglue, put the stones inside the doll and then sew it closed.
15. Place your doll on your altar for three days; three times a day wave your hand or wand over it with your intention spoken aloud.
16. Put the doll in a hidden spot somewhere in the child's

room but out of reach. Up in a closet is one place that will protect the child. Chant:

> *I hide you in (child's name) room;*
> *Protect this child with great health;*
> *I cast the spell with tremendous stealth*
> *For all of the love nature can throw.*
> *Bless this child from head to toe.*
> *So mote it be.*

You can substitute the child's name for this child.

PROSPERITY SPELLS

Money spells work best when cast during a full moon. It is always smart to do your cleansing rituals and make sure to have clear intentions when you are doing magic to attract prosperity.

"MONEY GROWS ON TREES" SPELL

Materials

- String
- Green cloth
- 9 Coins
- Green candle
- Ground cinnamon
- Essential oil for prosperity sandalwood or ginger

Steps

1. Do some deep breathing and then place all of the above ingredients on your cleansed altar.

2. Spend however long it takes to make sure you have positive vibes for the ritual.
3. Anoint your green candle with the prosperity oil (follow the candle dressing process from Chapter One).
4. Put your candle in its holder or on a fireproof dish and place it on your altar.
5. Place the nine coins in a circle around the candle. While you are designing the circle with your coins, imagine you have already received the money, projecting your thankfulness.
6. Light the candle and speak the following money spell three times:

> *One coin here, nine coins there,*
> *I feel my wealth everywhere.*
> *I invite prosperity and monetary gain.*
> *I have no more financial pain.*
> *So mote it be.*

"MONEY OVER THE MOON" SPELL

This spell must be cast under a full moon. If you have a real silver coin, great; if not any silver-colored coin works just fine. Also, have on hand a silver or green cloth.

Steps

1. Position yourself under the moonlight
2. Place your coin on your cloth so that you can see the moonlight shining on it.
3. Gently wave your hands over the coin while imagining that you are gathering all of the silver in the moon.
4. Chant aloud:

Beautiful spirit of the Moon

Bring me prosperity soon.
Fill my till with all the gold.
As much as you have my hands can hold.
So mote it be.

"WITCH'S BOTTLE" SPELL TO SELL

Everything that goes into your witch's bottle is symbolic and all of it will attract customers to your product or service. This spell can only be performed during the new moon.

Materials

- Your business card x 2
- Clear tape
- 1 Pen
- Green ribbon
- Chocolate coins (the ones in the gold foil) or you can use real coins.
- 1 Bottle
- Honey

Steps

1. Draw a bumble bee on the back of your business card (bees are a symbol of prosperity; see diagram below).
2. On the back of the other business card, draw the sigil for good sales (see diagram below).
3. Roll the card up like a bill, put a green ribbon around it, and stick it in the bottle.
4. Add the chocolate coins (a symbol for the sale coming to you in a "sweet" fashion.) If you use real coins, cleanse them in the dirt overnight first.
5. Tape the card with the sigil for good sales across the front of the bottle.

6. Bury the bottle on the next full moon and draw a pentagram on top of the soil with the top point facing west. Leave the bottle undisturbed.

GARDEN GROWTH ELEMENTAL SPELL

You can ask any witch and they will tell you that their garden is one of life's most magical places. There are many books out there devoted only to magic and gardens. Witches whose spiritual journeys are earth-based start planning their gardens in the early months of spring. The very act of starting a new life from a seed is ritualistic magic at its best, let alone the magic of watching it go from seed to seedling to sprout and then blossom. This is literally watching magic unfold right in front of our very eyes. There are lunar gardens, magical herb gardens, goddess gardens, and more. This spell is for raising an elemental garden. Midsummer or Litha is a wonderful time to start digging your garden! The earth is warm and the sun is at its peak. What you are going to do here is connect specific sections of your garden with the four elements.

Steps

1. Keeping in mind this garden is going to be circular, consider the amount of space you have and drive a ceremonial stake into the ground right in the center.
2. Tie a piece of string to the top of the stake and begin marking your perimeter by walking around in a circle.

3. Mark your circle by sprinkling black soil or birdseed.
4. Now that your circle perimeter is marked, till or dig up the soil.
5. Standing in your soon to be elemental garden, face north.
6. Divide your circle into elemental sections, so that ¼ of the circle is devoted to the directions which coincide with the elements.
7. Take some rocks or stones of your liking and mark your sections.
8. Very carefully, start to choose your plants.
9. North is connected to the earth, which is associated with security and stability. Use honeysuckle and magnolia.
10. East is connected to air, which is associated with mental clarity and wisdom. Use plants in the mint family, such as sage and mugwort
11. South is connected to fire, which is associated with compassion and creativity. Plant basil and rosemary.
12. West is connected to water, which is associated with intuition and emotion. Plant chamomile and hyssop.
13. As you begin making holes for each plant, add blessings. Dig your hands into the soil feeling it and thanking it. You can create your own little song or chant. Plants love music. You can also give an offering to each section, such as fire for the south, water for the west, and so on. This is a sacred space, so smudging is entirely appropriate.
14. Add any spiritual accessories, statues, and keep in theme with each element. Cockleshells go well with water. They make any garden look magical.

"RAIN DANCE" SPELL

1. Cast a sacred circle outside in the afternoon around 4:00 pm.
2. Place a clear quartz crystal at the bottom of a glass or crystal bowl and fill with spring water.
3. Program the water and the crystal with your intention; specifically mentioning rain.
4. Cup some water in your hands and dance around your circle while spilling the water from your hands 5 times chanting or singing:

> ***Rain, Rain, come today!***
> ***With drops of water, come our way,***
> ***From the sky and over the land,***
> ***For you comes this water from my hands.***
> ***So mote it be.***

"RAIN, RAIN GO AWAY" STORM PROTECTION SPELL

Materials

- Goblet
- Wine
- White Candle
- Amber or Evergreen Incense
- Wooden spoon
- Collected, stored, and blessed rainwater (you can use your moon water, but it is good to have some protection water made from the rain).
- If you can leave a container out during a thunderstorm the rainwater will be charged from lightning, which makes for powerful magic water.

- If you do not have any collected rainwater, use consecrated water.

Blessed Water Instructions:

- Pour some spring water into a bowl.
- Pour some salt into the water and stir it with your hand three times in a clockwise direction.
- Wave your hands over the water and chant

> *I exorcise all negativity from this creature of water, both unseen and seen, and bless thee water in the name of the divine Goddess Amphitrite.*

Steps

1. Cast a sacred circle outside.
2. Light the candle and the incense .
3. Fill the goblet with a mixture of the blessed water and wine.
4. Starting at the East end of your property, take the wooden spoon and sprinkle the water along the perimeter of your property, around your car, and anywhere else you need protection from a storm. Sprinkle with the spoon. Chant:

> *Stormy weather, here is my offering.*
> *Reap not your fury upon this property,*
> *Nor my family, nor their possessions.*
> *So mote it be.*

5. Continue until you have come full circle.

6. Save a few drops of your potion for your altar and pour the rest out in the direction that the storm is coming from.

"CONFIDENCE IN ME" TEA

How many times in your life have you passed up an opportunity because you were so sure you either didn't deserve it or there was no chance you would be able to achieve it? Have you passed up chances to invest in your own small business or travel on a whim? Are there times you wish you had spoken up, but were too afraid of other people's reactions? After today, you can leave your insecurities and doubts behind and change your attitude radically. Going forward you will be confident enough to be the captain of your own ship of life thanks to a bit of magic, a few powerful crystals, and willingness of intent.

Ingredients

- Earth: Ginger root, lemon, rhodiola (boosts dopamine) or cinnamon.
- Water: The essence of your medium and the canvas carrying your magic.
- Air: The fragrances and steam arising from your potion.
- Fire: Your tea's warmth, giving you confidence.
- Spirit: All of the Elements combined in your ritual finalized with sipping your tea.

Steps

1. Keep in mind, one cup of tea will require at least one teaspoon (3 grams) of dried herbs. So, if you are making one cup of tea for 7 days in a row, you will need to blend at least 21 grams of herbs.
2. Spell out your recipe in your own handwriting. Create a name for your magical blend and pen down your intention. Feel free to add your own incantation.
3. Blend your herbs together, while speaking your

intention three times, raising the volume each time. Do it three more times, while making your voice softer each time until you have it internalized.

GOAL ACCOMPLISHMENT JAR SPELL

Materials

- Jar
- Cinnamon
- Basil
- Sage
- Rose oil
- Rosemary
- Rose quartz
- Pen and paper
- Bee drawing (see diagram in "Witch's Bottle Spell" to Sell)
- 1 Green candle

Steps

1. Light the green candle.
2. Rub some rose oil around the rim of the jar.
3. Start with a layer of sage clippings at the bottom of your jar.
4. Add a layer of cinnamon.
5. Add a layer of basil.
6. Write your goals or goal on your piece of paper.
7. Put your rose quartz in the center of the paper and fold it up.
8. Put the parcel in the jar.
9. Cover the paper with a layer of rosemary.
10. Put your bee drawing on top of the rosemary.

11. Put the top on and place the jar where you can regularly reflect upon it.
12. Blow out the candle to activate the spell.

"COMMUNICATION IS A TWO-WAY STREET" SPELL

Do you wish you knew how to communicate better with your significant other(s); that you knew how to say what you mean before you say something that can cause a disconnect between you? Do you suddenly find yourself in the middle of an argument without knowing how you got there? Are you having difficulty explaining yourself or expressing your feelings? Good communication requires mutual respect and effective listening. I created this spell to help ease communication efforts, but you have to be willing to listen to your loved one without preparing a rebuttal while they are talking. If you are thinking about what you are going to say when the other person is talking, it is impossible to hear them. Remain calm, cast this spell, and then listen.

Materials

- 3 Blue candles
- Lavender incense
- Amber oil
- Cell phone
- Dill
- Oregano
- Caraway

Steps

1. This spell should be cast at your altar if it is big enough, if not, the kitchen table will do just fine.

2. Light your lavender incense and put it in your abalone shell or a fireproof dish.
3. Light your blue candle.
4. Place your cell phone in the center of your altar or table.
5. Scatter the herbs and lavender buds in a circle around your cell phone.
6. You will need three candles, one for each day. Let them burn all the way down.
7. In a clockwise motion rub the amber oil on your throat and speak the spell three times and for three days.

> *Communication needs trust.*
> *Talking, we must.*
> *I'll speak to you.*
> *You'll speak to me.*
> *Communication with trust will be.*
> *So mote it be.*

"NEW LOVE SPELL" FOR BLESSING A RELATIONSHIP

The tingle of a new relationship can also cause angst. You may be worrying that things may go wrong. Whenever you cast a spell involving relationships, always seek permission from the other person. Otherwise, the magic can be considered a manipulation and backfire. For this spell you will have to put your kitchen witchery to the test.

1. Bake a loaf of bread.
2. In the moonlight, hold the loaf of bread up at the moon.
3. Ask the Lady Diana the Lunar Goddess to bless the bread and the new relationship.
4. While enjoying the moon with your new lover, tear a

piece of the bread (do not cut it with a knife) and share it with them.

"MEND A BROKEN HEART" SPELL

Throughout life, we experience a wide range of emotions and energies. One of the more painful experiences that can linger is a breakup. Taking the time to symbolize the meaning of these feelings through rituals allows us the ability to move past the pain and recover by moving and releasing negative or painful energies. Visualizing and imagination is a powerful tool that helps us to create our own reality. Consciously using our words or casting a spell can create more peace by speeding up the process. This is an in-depth spell for deep healing after a breakup.

Materials

- 1 white egg
- Lemon balm tea
- Essential rose oil
- 1 pink rose
- 1 pink candle
- Honey

Steps

1. Sit down in a quiet place where you will not have distractions.
2. Cup the egg in your hand.
3. Meditate on the ended relationship, paying close attention to your grief, frustration, loneliness, or other negative feelings, letting them come to the surface.
4. Do not fight the feelings; cry without fear or shame.

5. During this part of the ritual, gently roll the egg over your face.
6. Visualize the egg soaking up all of your unhappiness as if it were a sponge.
7. Once you feel the egg has soaked up all of your negative and painful emotions, take it as far away from your home as possible and bury it.
8. All of the unhappiness and depression projected into the egg will be neutralized when absorbed by the earth.
9. Return home and make some herbal tea with lemon and put in it a couple of rose petals and some honey.
10. Sit with your pink candle and place the rest of the rose petals in a circle around it.
11. As you are lighting the candle, imagine the rose petal scent connecting to the warmth of the candle filling you and the room with loving, beautiful, and warm lights with the sweet smell of rose.
12. Using some essential rose oil, anoint your heart chakra.
13. While sipping the tea, speak aloud:

Gentle tea with your healing art, warm my soul and soothe my heart. So Mote it be.

14. Visualize yourself surrounded and filled with peacefulness and love.

15. Know you deserve happiness and love and experience the weightlessness of being free from the past relationship.

16. Look into the flame of the candle and see your new life full of joy and happiness, fulfilled and healed; freed from the bondage of a bad relationship.

APHRODITE BEAUTY OIL

Ingredients

- 1 Ounce glass amber colored bottle with dropper
- 1 Tiny rose quartz crystal
- Jojoba oil as the base
- Almond oil ⅛ oz
- Vitamin E liquid ¼ oz
- Essential oils:
- Jasmine 15 drops
- Rose ⅛ oz
- Ylang ylang 20 drops

Steps

1. Cleanse your rose quartz by rolling it in salt a couple of times (the salt will charge it too).
2. Fill the bottle ¼ of the way with Jojoba oil.
3. Add liquid vitamin E.
4. Add almond oil.
5. Drop the crystal into the container.
6. Add essential oils.
7. Use daily,

BLACK OBSIDIAN AND CLEAR QUARTZ PROTECTION STONE DUO

Black obsidian crystals are powerful protection stones, and when amplified with a clear quartz crystal, they are even more powerful. Black obsidian obviously doesn't hide from dark energy. Instead it brings light to the darkness, strips negativity from your path, and directs you toward love. Black obsidian also has great healing properties, especially in times of personal loss. Clear quartz is the most powerful protection stone as it unblocks all of the chakras and amplifies the magic of other crystals.

Materials

- Clear quartz
- Black obsidian
- Sage plant

Steps

1. Bury both crystals in the soil of the sage plant for seven days.
2. Carry them both in your pocket for seven days.
3. Recharge them with either sage soil or by smudging as needed. You can use your intuition as a warning when your crystals start to carry negative weight. It is then time to cleanse and recharge them.

PROTECTION JAR SPELL

If you are a new witch or an experienced witch, at some point in your magical practice you should or already have come across a bottle loaded up with some very nice-looking things, such as blossoms, crystals, herbs, and salts, as well as some unusual looking items. such as spices, rusty nails, and olive oil. Maybe the jar had a top fixed by candle wax or a common artisan top. If you haven't come across a Mojo Jar, it is time to stop missing out on its intense powers. This particular Jar is mojo for protection. I love to look at it sitting on my altar and it makes a great conversation starter when people visit. This is a spell jar full of expectations and vitality that protects you from negativity. Here is how to make it.

Materials

- Pen and paper
- White candle
- Salt
- Jasmine
- White sage
- Chamomile
- Rosemary
- Rose petals

Steps

1. Everything you put into your Mojo Protection Jar should be placed in deliberately and carefully, totally expecting to oblige it. The reason for its existence is to put a bountiful source of security and wellbeing in your home or sacred space.
2. You can get your materials either from your garden or the grocery store.
3. Write your intention on your piece of paper finishing with "So Mote it Be."
4. Start layering your items according to your intuition with the message in the very middle so it is protected all around.
5. When your jar is full, light your candle and let some of the wax drip onto the jar's lid.
6. Let the candle completely burn down.
7. Recharge your jar every full moon by sitting it out under the full moon's reflection
8. Keep it where you can marvel at it but be careful not to place it where children can access it. The crystals can be a choking hazard and some jars or bottles you decide to create may have ingredients not fit for human consumption.

BANISH THE DARK SPELLS

Banishing spells are common techniques that should be cultivated by all witches. Whether banishing negativity, an unwanted spirit, an addiction, or a bad relationship, banishing provides you with the magic to clear and rid a circumstance you no longer want to have in your life and provides you with more control of what you do want in your life. The reason banishing is a foundational practice is because magic and life in general are full of uncertainties, so it is very important to learn how to protect yourself. It is an uncomfortable feeling for anyone to find themselves in a dark circumstance that they don't know how to escape; and in the world of magic, it's even worse. You really do not want to end up on the downside of another spirit or witch. The good news is you never have to be in that position. Learning how to defend yourself with magic and making your security a top priority goes a long way in providing you with the conviction you need to deal head on with any situation that arises. It is best to use banishing spells when you are in a calm and relaxed state of mind. If you're angry, your spell work can become hex-like, rather than banishing or merely ridding your life of the problem. Wiccans are very serious about never causing unintentional harm to anyone, as opposed to just having them removed from your life.

BANISH BY BURNING

Materials

- A pen
- 1 piece of paper
- Fireproof plate or bowl
- Work surface that is heat tolerable
- Matches

This is a simple yet effective spell to execute. Start out by penning your intention, namely whatever you are intending to banish (a personal character defect such as procrastination or negative self-dialog, the name of someone or some spirit, etc.). It may be obvious, but safety first when working with smoke and fire.

1. Spend five or ten minutes focusing on what is written on your piece of paper, call out your intention as precisely as you can to whichever spiritual guide you feel faith in for this specific spell.
2. Simply, light your piece of paper on fire and drop it onto your plate.
3. While it is burning, imagine your selected target vanishing from your life and then zero in all of your imagination on how your life is like without it, as if it has already happened.
4. Once the paper is finished burning, gather the ashes and throw them outside of your house. Toss them to the wind or put them in the outside trash but do it right away.

BANISH BY CANDLE

Materials

- 1 candle holder with 1 **black** candle
- Anointing oil of your preference
- Matches
- Paper
- Salt
- Cayenne pepper
- Scribing or carving tool

Steps

1. Slowly scatter your salt in a circle, moving counterclockwise around you and your workspace, while imagining a salt barrier for your protection while casting your spell.
2. Call out your intention and scribe it into your candle. For instance you may carve "My fear is gone" or "Larry is out of my life." You may also want to carve a banishing symbol (sigil) into your candle.
3. When you have concluded your carving, conduct your anointment with whichever oil you feel is right for the spell.
4. Sprinkle cayenne pepper over your candle.
5. Light your candle while reciting your intention aloud into a chant or mantra while your candle is burning.
6. Let the candle burn all the way down. Make sure it is sitting safely on a fireproof surface and that your pets don't singe a whisker, too.

"There's the Door" Spell for Banishing a Toxic Person from Your Life

Materials:

- Scissors
- 2 black candles
- Cayenne pepper
- 1 piece of paper or photo of the person you wish to banish.

Cast when the moon is waning for best results.

Steps

1. Light both candles.
2. Write the person's name on a piece of paper and find a

photo of that person (try to get a photo, it makes the spell very strong).
3. Place the photo and the name between the two black candles.
4. Sprinkle cayenne over the flames
5. Speak the following spell,

> ***May "name of the person" be kept away from me.***
> ***Now be gone so I can be free.***
> ***From this place "name" will depart, forever we will be apart.***
> ***This is my spell and it is strong.***
> ***My life is good now that "name" is gone.***
> ***So Mote it be.***

6. Cut the photo and the paper in half and toss into the flame.

"SACRED CLEANSING WATER" RECIPE

Steps

1. Get a large clean glass bowl and fill it ¾ of the way full.
2. Sprinkle sea salt into the water, use your intuition as to the amount.
3. Put a clear quartz in the water.
4. Place the bowl under a full or waxing moonlight overnight.
5. Pour the water into a glass bottle, that you have smudged and anointed with either sweet orange, patchouli, or cinnamon essential oil.

"REMOVING EVIL FROM AN OBJECT" SPELL

Without a doubt, every object in your home or office holds the energy that was placed in it by you or someone else. Sometimes, we either purchase or are gifted an object that has energy embedded within it. In general, the energy is good or neutral, but what if it is bad or negative energy? There are times when we have those items in our possession and something bad has happened. You don't want to have to get rid of those objects, but they can be awful reminders of something bad. Other times, there is some ominous feeling about a random object you own. No one wants ominous energy in home or at their workplace. Well, here is what you do:

Steps

1. The object must be smudged or cleansed or the bad, negative, or even evil energy can permeate your home or office, which is the last thing you need.
2. Call upon the elements and deities to grant positive attributes, vibrations, or energies to the object you have cleansed and now need to bless.
3. It always comes down to you to set a positive intention for the object. Without a purpose, you can't assume a blessing spell will work.
4. Imagine the object glowing in a white light.
5. Bless your object with positive vibrations. Chant:

> ***Goddesses and God of this object,***
> ***I ask you to bless this item and give it the power to make good between us.***
> ***Protect it from darkness while I sleep.***
> ***So Mote it be.***

BANISHING SIGIL

A sigil is a symbolic representation of your intention that you create to change your circumstances and manifest your desires. Sigils seem simple but are extremely powerful.

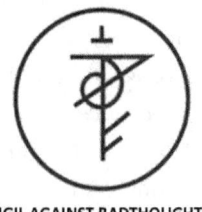 

SIGIL AGAINST BADTHOUGHTS   **I AM PROTECTED FROM NEGATIVE ENERGY**

Steps

1. To banish bad spirits from your home, bad thoughts from your head, and lust from your mind you can use banishing sigils. You can practice drawing these sigils above, if you are just starting out. Remember, everything in spellcasting is about intention and intuition, so learning how to develop yours will define the strength of your spells.
2. Cut out the sigil you have drawn and hold it your hands while visualizing your mind, home, or heart filling up with its energy and gleaming light around the exterior of your doors (if you are banishing negativity from your home) or glowing brightly around an object (if you are banishing evil from an item).
3. When you are finished your banishing spell, burn it in an abalone shell or fold it up and put it behind a mirror.

"WALK AWAY YOUR TROUBLES" SPELL

This simple and effective spell makes perfect sense!

Materials

- 1 piece of chalk, chosen by your own decision
- Your walking shoes

Steps

1. Using the piece of chalk, write what you wish to banish on the bottom of your shoes or sneakers.
2. Go for a stroll or wear them throughout the day and with every step you take imagine your problem disappearing at the same time as the chalk disappears.

ANCESTRAL COMMUNION SPELL

Everyone wants to communicate with their ancestors, every now and then. Sometimes, it is for comfort and sometimes for advice. Worshiping our ancestors is a very common form of religious and spiritual practice across the globe. As witches, we use meditation and rituals to get our ancestors to come to the table and lend us some of their insight. How we sense their presence is by our intuition. Their wisdom on death and life is a very valuable resource for any Wiccan. This spell, when cast, allows you to communicate rather easily with your ancestors even if you are not at your ancestor's altar. You must come into this ritual with a specific topic or question you want to discuss.

Materials

- Earth element offerings (meat, milk, water, and wine make good offerings)
- Graveyard pine or cedar incense

- 1 Abalone shell
- 8 Blue candles
- Crystal of your choice (if you know your ancestor's birthstone, use it)
- salt

Steps

> *Ancestors living so wild and free,*
> *Keep these gifts that come from me.*
> *I am inviting the most special one.*
> *To sit with me until we are done.*

1. Creating your own invocation is the best way because you know what you are trying to accomplish and should have the specifics. This is an example of a basic invocation just to give you an idea. Include the names of the ancestors you want to invoke.
2. This spell works best if you're out in nature. Your backyard is okay, but the more natural and wilder the area the more the essence of your ancestor can talk to you.
3. Create a sacred circle with your 8 blue candles burning around you.
4. Surround your candles with a circle of salt.
5. Light your incense.
6. Put your offering near the candles. It is their fire that delivers the offering.
7. Sit in a comfortable position, holding your crystal, and begin your unique ancestor invocation.
8. Visualize aspects related to your ancestry and start to say the name of the ancestor you are calling for a minimum of 8 times.
9. Meditate with closed eyes and pay close attention to sounds around you. The answers come in many forms,

so focus and notice any sounds or approaching animals. Or you can listen closely for the answer to come to your mind as a feeling or a decision.
10. When you feel answered, slowly open your eyes.
11. Look for responses from what you can see. You will know with your intuition what they are.
12. Close your circle and make sure to clean up afterward.
13. If the land belongs to you or the offering is biodegradable, you can leave it there. Otherwise dispose of it properly or burn it.
14. Put the crystal on your altar.
15. Continue to look for symbols and signs (feathers, dreams, rocks, unexpected phone calls) related to your ancestors throughout the day and on your way home.
16. Communication can last up to three or more days.

"I NEED CLOSURE" SPELL

There really isn't a notable factor in what provides us with a feeling of closure. If it is after the loss of a loved one, we have societal bereavement displays like wearing black, funeral ceremonies, and "sitting shiva." But healing has to take place within us before we can move on and gain our peace of mind back. This spell is for closure after a loss or a breakup. It also works for any situation that has come to an end, such as a court case or graduation. It takes only around 25 minutes.

Materials

- 1 Bowl or cauldron of water
- Vanilla
- Rosemary
- 3 Teaspoons of Epsom salts
- Garnet or rose quartz crystal

Steps

1. In your mind's eye, visualize a doorway with a dark corridor leading away from it, while cupping the crystal in your hands.
2. Imagine the door slowly closing and speak aloud:

> ***This is just a passage,***
> ***Not a place to keep.***
> ***This is where no one goes.***
> ***This door is now and forever closed.***
> ***So Mote it be.***

3. Stir the herbs and salt in a counterclockwise fashion into the cauldron.

4. Place your crystal in the cauldron and leave it there for 15 minutes.

5. Remove the crystal from the cauldron, take it far from your home to a crossroad, and bury it. You can also throw the stone as far away from you as you can and you will have closure, but burying it seals the deal.

SEA SAGE CLEANSING

As we age, so do our homes, and over time, negative energy can build up. Consider that every argument, physical illness, bad mood, and any other negative happenings lead to the "bad juju" airing around your home and property. So, whether you have lived in your home for many years, or just moved in, it's best to stick to the old rule of "cleanliness is next to godliness." This is a tried-and-true method for keeping your surroundings happy, healthy, and negativity free!

Steps

1. Firstly, start with taking a spiritual bath or shower yourself. It is not an absolute necessity, as you have to smudge yourself anyway, but it is the best way to improve your magic.

2. Smudge yourself first. Speak aloud:

> ***Smoke of sage encompass me, casting away negativity.***

3. Smudge each room of the home. Repeat the chant at the back door and front door of your home with the door open while making a sweeping out motion with your hands.

4. Go back to the room where you began and start salting the home. Sea salt or regular salt works.

5. Sprinkle the salt starting with the corners and outer walls.

6. Repeat the chant in every corner and keep chanting until you salt-circle the home and finish at the back or front door.

7. Say the final chant:

> ***So Mote it be.***

INVOCATION OF HECATE

This spell is to invoke Hecate, the ancient goddess of witchcraft, magic, necromancy, night and moon. For us, her name itself is a symbol of empowerment, mystery, and magic and causes deep rumbling within our very souls. She has a complex history, also known as the Keeper of the Keys that open the doors to our souls, and the Breaker of Chains to break whatever ties bind us. Invoking Hecate during times of struggle or stress feels uniquely supportive. This spell is to call upon

Hecate to break the chains that bind you and open the door to your soul.

Materials

- 1 Key
- 2 White candles
- Torches
- Sage
- Bay leaf
- Frankincense
- Myrrh
- Fruit
- Nuts
- Smoked fish (optional)

Steps

1. This spell is best done out in nature and on the ground, where the earth is exposed.
2. Cast a sacred circle.
3. Light two white candles on each side of your sacred circle.
4. Place your offerings next to one of the candles.
5. Next to the other candle, place the key.
6. Put the herbs over the key.
7. Pick up the key and hold it over your heart.
8. Chant while holding the key to your heart:

> *I call upon you Hecate, Breaker of Chains,*
> *Keeper of Keys to bless this night with a*
> *   sacred rite*
> *and bind your wisdom with this key, that I may*
> *   wear for eternity.*

9. Put the key around your neck and partake in ½ of the offering, symbolizing breaking bread with the Goddess Hecate.

10. Raise one of the candles toward the East with your left hand while waving your right hand over the earth and chant:

> ***O most faithful Hekate, goddess of night,***
> ***who knows my secrets and my plight***
> ***and comes to help me with my spells***
> ***accept my offering that from within me dwells.***

11. Turn this ritual into a party or a feast. Use only natural light, play music, dance, do magic! Let your happiness shine in front of Hecate and any other gods, goddesses, or spirits who decided to attend. There is no need to close the circle because you want the spirit(s) invoked in this ritual to wander your home with their wisdom and protection.

INVOCATION OF NYX

As the Goddess of the night, Nyx lives in the depths of the underworld, of Hades. She perfectly personifies the night, as she is a shadowy figure and has been depicted as winged, crowned, and as a charioteer. She is unique in that she can influence humans in both good ways and bad. It is said that Nyx was the only goddess feared by Zeus because she was stronger and older than him. She is honored by the crystal Moonstone and she should be called upon during a full moon. Nyx is associated with all things about the night.

Materials

- Sage
- Black salt (you can burn a stick and use the ashes to make black salt)
- White tealight candles

- 1 Purple candle
- 1 Green candle (earth)
- 1 Blue candle (water)
- 1 Yellow candle (air)
- 1 Red candle (fire)
- Myrrh incense

Steps

1. Cast your circle with candles.
2. Place the purple candle in the middle, as it represents Nyx.
3. Call the elements.
4. Light the purple candle.
5. Call out:

Nyx of the Night, come to me!

7. When you feel her presence start to chant or sign the invocation:

> *Because of you I see the night through.*
> *Because of you I sleep the night through.*
> *Because of you I cherish the night.*
> *Because of you I am safe and sound in the darkness.*
> *It is you, the Goddess of the Night,*
> *That has me rest easy in the darkness.*
> *It is you, oh Goddess of the night,*
> *that sees me through my darkest times.*
> *I thank you, oh sweet Goddess of the Night,*
> *for all of your blessings and your might.*

8. Thank each element and close your circle.

BONDING WITH A FAMILIAR

You have probably been raised to believe that most witches have black cats as pets. In reality, witches bond with a specific animal that they have a spiritual and personal connection with. Often, the familiar lives with the witch and is helpful in crafting spells and providing spiritual favors. The Native American also refers to familiars as a species of animal the practitioner has certain traits in common with. Your familiar should symbolize something inherent to you. Something you know down deep about yourself that cannot be explained but is understood by your familiar is included in this bond. For instance, rather than your pet dog sharing an inherent trait with you, maybe a wolf does. Shy people might prefer a turtle or cat, while more assertive people might better identify with bulls or oxen. People who very much enjoy nighttime activities may feel strongly connected to owls or bats. For the sake of this book, let's talk about bonding with animals that are domesticated. I wouldn't want anyone to get hurt trying to interact with wild animals, nor do I want the animal hurt or removed from its natural habitat.

CHOOSING YOUR FAMILIAR

This is a very serious matter so please take into careful consideration if you have the money, the time, and the commitment it takes to train a familiar. Having said that, it is an incredibly rewarding spiritual relationship. First off, your main obligation is to give the animal a safe and optimal quality of life, so think about practicalities. More often than not, you will be chosen by an animal familiar. Rather than going and looking for a familiar, try putting your intention out there and see who comes along.

HOW TO CALL A FAMILIAR

1. Cast a sacred circle and light candles and incense.
2. Take your pulse to find your rhythm.
3. Beat on a drum to match the rhythm of your heart so that the familiar that may come along knows your rhythm. Do this for 5 minutes.
4. Now that the energy is raised, chant in beat with your heart:

> *I call upon a beast.*
> *A beast calls upon me.*
> *We will dance together,*
> *to the beat of our hearts.*
> *Feather, scale, skin, or fur,*
> *Come to me, my familiar!*

5. Stop hitting the drum with the last words of the chant and imagine the animal.

6. If nothing happens, be patient. You may have a dream or a random animal may cross your path; just keep your intention open.

Once you think you have met a good option as a potential "candidate" here are some activities to deepen your relationship:

1. Try synchronizing the rhythm of your breathing by letting your animal get close enough (using common sense of course). For instance, if it is a cat, you can let the familiar sit on your chest so you can see and feel the rhythm of its breathing. Then try to match your rhythm of breathing. This is how you sync your

energies and gain a better understanding of your familiar empathetically.
2. Use your crystals to soothe your familiar. It shouldn't replace regular veterinary care, but their healing energies can't hurt. It's also a great way to practice your skills.
3. If your familiar is a cat or a dog, take it on a nature walk. Make sure to use a leash, as required. It will be great for you both.
4. Use your familiar's fur or shedding in your spells. It will greatly enhance your magic because they belong to a being that you care so much for.
5. Adorn your familiar with crystals and sigils in their collar. Cast a protection spell on the collar by letting it charge in the moonlight or smudging it. Rosemary smudging is a great protective barrier with high vibrational energy.
6. Include your familiar in your sacred circle. First, try waiting for it to enter on its own or call it in. Remember, it is here for you to learn from it, not the other way around.
7. Conduct a sacred massage or use kitchen witchery on the familiar's food.
8. Once you have bonded, conduct a dedication ritual.

3

RED MAGIC SPELLS HOODOO

Red magic is a very potent type of spell work as it involves intense emotions, passion, attention seeking, sexuality, and lust. It also works well for helping you through a bad breakup and boosting your confidence. However, remember that red is also the color of violence and rage and therefore should be practiced respectfully and carefully (Greenwood, 2014).

WHAT IS HOODOO/FOLK MAGIC

Folk magic includes various types of magical practices from many diverse perspectives that are connected only by the fact that they are practiced by common folk. They are not necessarily ceremonial rituals practiced by the more experienced witches. It is usually pragmatic by nature, designated to tend to the common ills of society, such as love, luck, healing, banishing, finding lost people or items, blessing the harvests, granting parenthood or fertility, and so on. Folk magic employs often simple ways that change over time. Materials used are readily available, such as twine, crystals, feathers, coins, herbs, nails, eggs, and plants.

Hoodoo is a type of black magic that started during the nineteenth century. It is a mixture of European, Native American, and African folk magic. It is commonly strongly rooted in Christian imagery. Christian Bible phrases are commonly used in magical rituals, and the Bible itself is thought of as a powerful item, capable of driving away negative forces. Hoodoo is also known as Rootwork, and despite sounding similar, it has nothing to do with Voodoo or Vodou.

American folk magic includes the Pow-Wow. Native American in origin, Pow-Wow is practiced by the people from the Pennsylvania Dutch communities. Also known as hex-work, Pow-Wow uses hex signs. These are also available to buy as trinkets, but don't have any magical power. Pow-Wow is usually practiced for protection. Often hex signs are placed on barns for protection from danger. Pow-Wow also uses Christian concepts. Mary and Jesus invocations are commonly used in incantations.

Here are the properties of red magic:

- Its Season is summer.
- It is associated with the number 1.
- Its zodiac Sign is Aries.
- Its planet is Mars.
- It is a fire element.
- Its direction is south.
- Its day is Tuesday.
- Holidays associated with it are Yule, Beltane, and the Lunar New Year.
- Its animals are the lion, tiger, wolf, and bear.
- Its crystals are all the red stones: rubies, red tourmalines, red topazes, garnets, red jaspers.
- Its magical uses include sexuality, passion, lust, all things related to blood and healing, transformation, and action, among others.

"LOVE BELL" SPELL

A witch's bell is a force to be reckoned with! Bells are used to invoke the Elements and various deities. Spirits of evil flee from the high-pitched clear sounds bells make, especially when sounded with intent. Where you find your bell(s) is up to your intuition. You can buy a new one or look for a used one at a garage sale. It's nice to have many bells with differing tones, but for this "Love Bell" Spell, you only need one. Friday is the day of Venus, so it is the best day to cast this spell. You also want to cast this spell when there is a new moon or a full moon. This is when love spells are at their most potent.

Materials

- Witch's Bell
- 2 pink candles
- Pink rose petals
- 1 Garnet Crystal
- 1 Rose Quartz Crystal
- Palo Santo smudging bundle

Steps

1. Imagine a clear picture of who you want to cast this spell upon. Meditate on it for a while. There are many witches who have haphazardly cast love spells just to turn around and try to undo them.
2. Place your candles with the rose quartz and garnet crystals in the middle.
3. Light the candles.
4. Light your Palo Santo bundle and place it in a fireproof dish or abalone shell.
5. Pass your bell over the candle and through the smoke.
6. Ring the bell three times

7. Chant:

> *Bells are ringing for Aphrodite tonight.*
> *Crystals of love shimmering bright.*
> *I cast this spell, red with fire,*
> *Bring the love my heart desires.*
> *So Mote it be.*

8. Ring the bell three times each day for a week, while summoning Aphrodite and repeating the chant.

9. Carry the two crystals touching each other at all times in your pocket or pouch until your desire is met.

"LOVE KNOT" SPELL

Well, what could be a more significant symbol of love than "tying the knot"! Knots have deep significance in magic, partly due to their beautiful and simple symmetry. Very often knots are used for protection spells but in this case, you will be casting a love knot spell. The key to knot magic is using a length of 9. This can be either nine inches or nine feet. Always tie an uneven number of magical knots. If you know the person with whom you are casting the love spell, you can use their birthday. The length will be represented by the month and the number of knots will be represented by the day. If your love knot spell is for longevity of marriage, you can use the wedding anniversary with the same format.

Materials and Steps

- 3 Cords of yarn or string; you can pick your favorite romantic colors: red (passion), white (purity), and pink (love).
- Tie one knot at the end of one of the cords and imagine new love coming into your life. Chant:

> *Venus, Goddess of romance and love,*
> *Bring me love, sent from you above.*
> *So Mote it be.*

- Braid all three pieces of yarn together while imaging your love deepening with mutual respect.
- Tie another knot and repeat the chant.
- Continue to imagine your love in-depth; think of kissing, holding each other, happiness.
- Tie another knot and then another until you have seven knots and have chanted seven times.
- You can make this into a bracelet or carry it in your pocket but keep it on you until the spell has manifested.

LOVE POTION #9 PASSION TEA APHRODISIAC

This love potion is an herbal aphrodisiac that will nourish, excite, elevate, and sustain your sensual or sexual desires. Herbs have magical properties for physical, mental, and spiritual wellness. The healing and wellness properties of herbs include:

- Balancing hormones.
- Strengthening reproductive organs and surrounding tissues.
- Calming stress and anxiety.
- Promoting sexual stamina and vitality.
- Providing added energy.
- Exciting olfactory senses.
- Increasing fertility for both men and women.
- Nourishing the heart and liver.
- Increasing blood flow.

Before you conjure up your spell, try a single herb for two

weeks to see if you notice any connection. Remember, each herb has its own unique magical properties.

INGREDIENTS OF LOVE POTION #9

- 4 Organic green tea bags or chamomile tea bags
- 3 Pinches of nutmeg
- 1 Pinch of cloves
- 1 Pinch of rosemary
- 8 Fresh rose petals
- 3 Fresh mint leaves
- 3 Cups spring water
- 3 lemon leaves or 1 tablespoon fresh squeezed lemon
- Raw honey

Steps

1. Boil the spring water
2. Make sure that you do this on a Friday and there is a new moon.
3. Combine all of the ingredients in a teapot.
4. Pour boiling water over the leaves, petals, herbs and tea bags.
5. Add honey; approximately 3 tablespoons or to personal taste.
6. Let steep for 30 minutes.
7. Add honey to sweeten and chant:

> ***By the light of the moon I brewed this tea,***
> ***For a love spell to come over me.***
> ***Love is here to ring my bell,***
> ***With love intentions I cast this spell.***
> ***So mote it be.***

8. On the next Friday, make another batch of Love Potion #9 and give a cup to the person you are interested in. Love will surely follow.

"BATHING IN SENSUALITY" APHRODISIAC SPELL

Chuparosa or hummingbird oil comes from a desert shrub with tubular yellow, orange, and red flowers. It is referred to as hummingbird oil because it attracts hummingbirds to suck on its nectar. Well, that pretty much explains why it is an aphrodisiac! You can buy it online. If you just can't get your hands on it, you can use honeysuckle, lotus, or rose oil.

Ingredients

- Chuparosa or honeysuckle oil
- Himalayan pink salt
- 4 Gems; pick your partner's birthstone or use aquamarine. Remember, clear quartz crystals can substitute for all crystals.
- Lavender flower buds

Steps

1. Make your bathing room a sacred space. Place some flowers and candles around the tub and smudge the room in all corners.

2. Set your gems up around the tub.

3. As you're filling the tub, meditate on how the water is flowing and occupying space.

4. Speak aloud your intention:

> ***I am in the mood for some great love making.***
> ***I am releasing all inhibitions.***

5. Slowly pour in the pink Himalayan bath salts and the essential oils.
6. Gently breathe in their aroma and notice any sensations in your body.
7. Notice the change in the water when you added the salt.
8. Take a handful of lavender buds and whisper to them your intention.
9. Scatter the flower buds into the water.
10. Slip into the bathtub or hot tub.
11. Close your eyes and take in the heightened sensations.
12. Practice creative visualization of your sexual intention.
13. Wave your hand slowly through the water and envision the cleansing of your body.
14. Cross your fingers with the fingers on your other hand and put your hands over your heart.
15. Take nine deep breaths imagining the white light entering your body with each inhale.
16. Visualize your heart spilling white light outward, creating a sphere of sensuality around you. Envision your heart radiating, shining light throughout your body and outwards, creating a sphere of love and healing around you.
17. When you feel totally ready, let the water drain.
18. STAY IN the tub until all the water has left and feel the clear and empty space.
19. Leave with your body both clean and naked.
20. Express your gratitude aloud to the elements, plant spirits, and deities.
21. Make sure to drink 8 oz of fresh spring water after the ritual.
22. Ready yourself for what comes next.

CANDLE CARVING RITUAL (SCRIBING)

Looking for a forever soulmate or still figuring out that you have to love yourself first, before you can love another? This powerful spell is a bit complicated even though the materials are fairly simple. Please brush up on the elements' corresponding cardinal directions in the first chapter. Scribing or carving your intention on your candle involves using sigils, names, numbers, key words, among others. Once again, this spell is all about your intuition and intention. You can use the tip of your wand, a ritual knife, or a pin. Whichever instrument you choose, smudge and charge it before scribing. The key is to carve your candle with an image of something with great meaning to you or your ritual.

Materials

- 4 Red jarred candles
- 2 White jarred candles
- Scribing tool
- Rose essential oil

Steps

1. Carve into your candle words or symbols denoting your intent.
2. Meditate on your intention while carving. Below is the Sigil for attraction, but you can use any method of carving as long as you use a sacred tool.
3. Create a sacred circle in a place safe for lighting

candles. Place the four red candles, one in each cardinal point.
4. Light your north candle while invoking the earth.
5. Turning clockwise, light your east candle while invoking the air.
6. Light your south candle while invoking the fire.
7. Light your west candle while invoking the water.
8. While turning back to the north, light the first white candle just to the left of you and light the other white candle just to the right of you.
9. Speak aloud your intention each time you light a candle.
10. Put one drop of rose oil into each red candle.
11. While gazing at the flames rising up and staying steady, repeat your intention.
12. Pick up a white candle in each hand and tilt them toward each other, until they fuse into one flame; project your intention into the flame.
13. Close your circle by blowing out the candles in the reverse order they were lit (W-S-E-N).
14. Bury both white candles in the earth in an area you visit frequently. The soil will nurture your intention, bringing it to fruition.

"LETTING GO OF A LOVER" SPELL

This spell combines healing and cleansing, since you want to heal from the letting go process, as well as becoming strong enough to move ahead. This is not a quick spell, like some in this book, as letting go of a lover is one of the most challenging situations a person can face. Give yourself time to grieve and cry over your loss, as both are healing and purifying in nature. It is all a part of the letting go process and finding your way back to peace, joy, and happiness. This spell should be cast at the start of the waning moon. It takes an entire week to manifest.

Materials

- Blade
- 1 Purple pillar candle
- 2 White pillar candles

Steps:

1. Thoroughly smudge your sacred space and for best results have your candles charged either by sunlight, moonlight, crystal, or sage.
2. At your altar, place your candles in the form of a triangle with purple at the top and the two white candles at the bottom. The purple candle symbolizes your spiritual self, and the white candles symbolize you and your lover. White represents purity and will dissipate any negative energy that was between you and your lover.
3. While picturing your best qualities in your mind, light the white candle representing you. Do the same for the other candle, except remember the best about your lover, while imagining the flame burning away the worst.
4. Light the purple candle and meditate on you and your lover at your best. This will resonate deeply within you and help you to let go when you're ready. It seems like the opposite would be true but sadness, anger, and hate weigh heavily on your spiritual and emotional vibrations. If your anger and resentments are too strong at the beginning of the spell, smudge some more, especially around your white candles.
5. When you feel grounded and calm, snuff out your

candles, starting with the purple candle, then your lover's candle and, finally, your own.

6. Repeat this for seven days, and as the candles dwindle away, so will your burden; serenity and peace will take its place.

APHRODITE SEA CHARM

Known as the goddess of beauty and love in Greek mythology, Aphrodite is honored by many witches today. Venus, the goddess of love, is her equivalent in Roman mythology. This wonderful spell needs to only be cast once, and then you can use it on a daily basis. Each morning dap your neck, elbows, wrists, and your ears with this concoction.

Ingredients

- 1 Small jar
- 1 ½ Teaspoons beeswax pellets
- 2 Drops rose oil
- 2 Teaspoons vitamin E oil
- ¼ Cup almond oil
- 2 Drops vanilla oil
- 2 Drops sweet orange oil
- 2 Drops vanilla oil
- ⅛ Cup fine sea salt

Steps

1. Place 2 cups of water in your cauldron or saucepan.
2. Put the heat to medium and add the almond oil and beeswax and let them melt.
3. Take out the melted ingredients and add the vitamin E and essential oils, stirring with a sacred wooden stick or blessed popsicle stick.

4. Let the balm slightly cool but not harden.
5. Stir again and add it to your small jar and let sit until completely hardened.
6. Place your jar on your altar and light a candle.
7. Call upon the Goddess Aphrodite to favor your creation, chanting:

> ***Aphrodite, Goddess of beauty and love, I ask that you bless my creation , as it is crafted in your honor. So mote it be.***

8. Before using, rub your hands together to warm your fingers and then apply it.

"ADORATION CANDLE" SPELL

Anointing and burning red candles will put you in touch with your carnal pleasures, as the color red is associated with passion, pleasure, and love. An adoration candle will stimulate your personal power, energy, and vitality. It is also a good spell if a woman is trying to conceive. You can unleash your pure animal magnetism by casting this powerful spell. Cast in on a Friday.

Ingredients

- 2 Red candles
- Rose oil

Steps

1. Scribe your name on one of the candles and the name of your lover on the other. If you don't yet know the name of that person, scribe "beloved" or "true love."
2. Place the candles on both sides of your altar.

3. The next day at 7:00 pm scribe a love word, such as "faithful" or "devoted" on both candles.
4. Light the candles and speak your intention. Focus on your scribed word for the day. Picture yourself in the arms of that person, loving them, feeling them, and wanting them.
5. Picture the feelings being reciprocated.
6. Snuff out the candle and chant:

So mote it be.

1. Every evening at 7:15 pm scribe another love word into the candles and move them a bit closer to each other
2. Do this for seven days.
3. On the seventh day, the candles should be closer together. Let them burn all the way down.
4. If any wax is left, scratch it up and scatter it in a place you love, while concentrating on your spell.

HATHOR'S BATH RITUAL

Hathor was an Egyptian goddess like no other. There were more temples built to honor Hathor (2686 BC) than even the goddess Isis! She brings protection, good health, passion, and love and is symbolized by the stars and the sky. She governs water and gives birth to the morning sun. Hathor was connected to the Nile River and all water in general. If you're looking to bring more passion into your life, this is the spell to garnish a magical connection with Hathor and perform a bathing ritual in her honor.

Ingredients

- 1 Gallon Coconut Milk
- Rose oil

- Lavender oil
- Rose petals
- 1 Red candle
- 1 Pink candle
- 1 White candle

Steps

1. Place the candles near the tub and anoint them with rose oil.
2. Fill the tub with warm water.
3. Add the coconut milk and essential oils.
4. Scatter the rose petals in the water, saying:

> *Hathor, who lives in Thebes, hears me! I invoke thee, to come to me so I can adore and communicate with thee. O, beautiful Goddess Hathor, I thank thee for your protection. So mote it be.*

BIRCH BARK LOVE SPELL

Birch Bark is known as the "White Lady of the Woods,'" for it is a tree of great beauty and strength. Birch bark is associated with a renewal of vows and renewal of life and love because every spring it is one of the first trees to sprout new leaves. Birch is also associated with purification, fertility, and inception. Its purification properties are due to it being a natural antiseptic. Its element is water and its crystal is the emerald. Traditionally used for Wiccan Maypoles and Beltane fires, birches are the twigs of the Witch's besom.

> *Birch into the fire goes, in sign of what the Lady knows.*

Steps

1. Find a birch tree you can sit against; if there are none, you can buy birch bark from several witchery shops online.
2. Get to know the beautiful birch and ask its permission to peel some bark.
3. Place the bark on your altar and center your intention while waving your hand around it and smelling its scent.
4. Carry the bark with you and show it to the person you want to attract.
5. Ask them if they enjoy the aroma.
6. If they say they do not, they are not the right person.
7. If they do enjoy the aroma, it is a great way to start a conversation.
8. Be patient, as many will love the aroma, so you'll have to use your intuition to gauge the intensity of your connection with the person and the birch.

REVERSE LOVE SPELL

This Reverse Love Spell was created to undo the effect of an original love spell. This particular spell will revert the love spell to the condition that existed before it was cast.

Steps

1. Hold a mirror facing away from you and speak aloud:

> ***Circle of protection,***
> ***Realm of reflection,***
> ***May this love begone,***
> ***Feel the magic of this charm.***
> ***So mote it be.***

2. Smudge your entire home with white sage.

3. Scatter salt around your doors and then sweep it outside.

4. Burn a black candle at both ends while standing in front of a mirror to reverse the spell.

ATTRACTION POPPET

An attraction spell poppet is not at all difficult to make. Follow this guide and invite a bit of romance into your life with the charming attraction spell.

Materials

- Pink fabric ⅛ of a yard
- Scrap paper
- Cotton
- Scissors
- Needle
- Pink thread
- Dried rosemary, lavender, and roses

Steps

1. Either use scrap fabric or choose a fabric based on your intuition. It is best to pick a fabric that is 100% cotton. This spell poppet employs the principles of sympathetic magic and is sometimes referred to as a "Voodoo doll," but that phrase has been given a bad rap by Western culture. For this reason we will call it a spell poppet.

2. Traditionally, a spell poppet is used to fulfill positive endeavors, and in this case, your spell poppet will attract love. Much like the child protection poppet in the last chapter, spell poppets can also draw good luck and money.

3. On your scrap paper draw the image of your poppet. Here is an example of how basic it can be, for those of you who don't enjoy sewing:

4. Cut out your drawing and outline it on your fabric.

5. Cut the shape twice or double your fabric when you cut it.

6. Sew the poppet together leaving the bottom open for stuffing.

7. Stuff your Attraction Spell Poppet with the herbs and cotton.

8. Write your intention on a piece of nice stationary and put it into the poppet.

9. Adorn your poppet with a love sigil. You can use a red marker and make it look really nice, or you can glue crystals right on to the poppet. Get creative.

10. Charge your poppet by either sleeping with it overnight, smudging it, using a full moon, placing it in a sacred circle of crystals for several hours, or any of the other charging methods you know or learned in this book.

4

SORCERY/HEX SPELLS

People often ask about sorcery or black magic. In spite of all of the debates, magic is magic and really only uses colors to create spells. Hollywood, mass media, and the gaming industry have made black magic very popular. White is portrayed as good, red is portrayed as love, green is portrayed as money, blue is portrayed as calming, and black is portrayed as evil. This color-coding can be very helpful when designing your own Book of Shadows or spell casting code.

As previously stated, it is your intention that makes the magic. Some Wiccans consider black magic as spells which try to manipulate free will and can be dangerous if they return to you by the Rule of Three. As with all magic spells, you should do your homework and take care in considering your intentions. Some consider the negativity associated with black magic has racist vibes. Many of the black magic rituals are traditionally of Hoodoo, a type of African folk magic.

CEREMONIAL MAGIC

Ceremonial magic is a branch of witchery that relies predominantly on book learning. It involves complicated, precise rituals, in complex sets of relationships. Very much grounded in Judeo-Christian religiousness up until late in the 19th century, it is not uncommon for ceremonial magicians to continue to practice within that context even today. Another word for ceremonial magic is high magic. Its purpose is meant to be spiritual in nature, rather than pragmatic. It is about gaining purification, divine knowledge, attracting appropriate influences and embracing their destiny, as well as soul improvement. Currently, there is plenty of information available publicly on the beliefs and practices of ceremonial magic or high magic. However, a review of the literature states that often there is incomplete information and that it is only through practicing and serious training that the secrets of ceremonial magic can be unlocked (Ezzy, 2006, Manning, 2014).

LEFT AND RIGHT HAND MAGIC

Briefly, left-hand magic is barred by many social conventions unless it is beneficial. Harsh warnings are issued about the consequences of any practice considered to be harmful. Satanic and Luciferian practitioners consider themselves to be on the left-hand track. A practitioner of right-hand magic lives outside of social accord and ignores taboos, sometimes feeling a heightened sense of power from breaking those conventions. Only magicians who think of themselves as right-hand practitioners generally use the terminology.

PROTECTION SPELL

Here is a powerful spell to protect you from spiritual losses, especially those shed from malevolent sources.

Materials

- Turmeric capsules
- Chalice
- Mango leaves

Steps

1. Take the turmeric orally. Turmeric creates a powerful bio magnetic field around you that is so strong that it cannot be penetrated by evil forces.
2. Fill your chalice with water and add mango leaves. Facing the east, stare into the water for 10 minutes. Keep the chalice on your altar until evening time and then pour it out in front of your home. Do this for 21 days. This protects you from the bad eye spell.

RUNE OF PROTECTION

When choosing your rune for protection let your intuition help you pick either Thurisaz or Algiz. Thurisaz symbolizes Thor's hammer of power, and it represents the conscious action of defense. It will also protect your work and bring you good luck. Upside down represents uncertainty, discouragement, and resistance. Algiz symbolizes discovery and is connected to self-protection and survival instincts. Its spiritual force creates a protective shield around you and will defend you from dangers and attacks on every level of being. You decide which one you need. It is best to use the rune at night, when it is strongest. Meditate on it just before bedtime and you will sleep better and feel safe and protected. Don't forget to use runes in their upright positions and let their energies protect you and spread their protection throughout you.

. . .

STEPS

1. Wear the rune as a necklace. This way your protection will be attached to your body, especially if you have to deal with a difficult person or situation. Having it touching your skin will create a shield of protection from the evil eye and negativity.
2. Create your own sigil for either Thurisaz or Algiz and carry it with you.
3. Use it in your spell or ritual practice. Keeping your rune in your hands while creating a sacred circle, cleansing an object on your altar and chanting three times the following incredibly powerful spell:

> *I call upon Thurisaz or Algiz (the one your picked),*
> *Be my shield of protection for all harm and danger,*
> *Shelter me from the storms of life.*
> *Keep me safe.*
> *So mote it be.*

PEPPER PENTACLE

Pentacle has been symbolic of witchery for over 9,000 years. The image is associated with how we interact with the word on five levels, represented by the five points on the star. The top point is the spirit symbol, and moving clockwise, each following point is a symbol of water, fire, earth, and air. The Wiccan Pentacle is always pointed upwards, as pointing it downwards (towards Hades) would make it a satanic symbol. Many witches simply hang the pentacle on their wall as a symbol of the craft. Making it yourself is a much more power-wielding magic. Putting together sticks and branches gathered from the forest or driftwood pieces gathered from the beach will harness the elements' powers and help you along your magical journey. Black pepper is used in rituals and spells to give you protection and banish negativity and negative people from your life. If you want to rid yourself of an annoying individual, or someone has caused you harm, use black pepper, which is connected to fire. When cast with a pentacle in a spell, the black pepper packs a very powerful punch of sorcery.

Materials

- Black pepper
- Sticks
- Twine or fabric
- Pen and paper
- Black candle
- 2 Pentacles; one drawn on paper and the other made naturally.

Steps

1. Gather your sticks and twigs in a natural setting such as next to a river, in the forest, on the beach, in your neighborhood, or in the desert.
2. Pick twigs or sticks that are as straight as you can find, light in weight, and the same length. Grab some extras so you can play with how they fit best into your pentagram.
3. Create a sacred circle and lay them out on the ground, forming a five-pointed star.
4. Have the fifth point oriented in an upward direction
5. Overlap and intersect the ends, reordering the sticks until they fit the way you want them to.
6. Gather some twine, using your intuition or use material that draws you to it.
7. Wrap the twine or material where the twigs intersect until tightly bound.
8. Wrap in a clockwise direction.

9. Tie the inside intersections in the center of your star, so that wherever two sticks intersect you have twine covering them.
10. Meditate on where you want to display the star (altar, garden, or some other place that you feel is your sacred space.

Steps

This spell works with just the drawn pentacle, but for an added boost of power, constructing a pentacle from things of nature is incredibly rewarding.

1. Light your black candle.
2. Draw a large pentacle on your piece of paper.
3. Write your intention in the middle of the star.
4. Create a border around the star in black pepper.
5. Drip the black candle wax over your intention until it is covered in black wax.
6. Let the candle continue to burn for at least an hour.
7. You now have a pepper pentacle sigil.
8. Leave your sigil in a sacred place where it will not be disturbed until the spell has manifested.

"SUMMON A STORM" SPELL

Materials

- Pentagram
- 1 Clear quartz crystal or wand
- 1 White candle and lighter

Steps

1. Place the candle in the center of your altar.
2. Place your crystal or want next to your candle.
3. Light the candle.
4. Take the lighter and start at the point of water on your pentagram. Moving in a clockwise direction, stopping at each point, speak aloud the name of each of the elements.
5. Complete the first circle and then continue until your come back to the water point:
6. Chant

> *I call on the Elements of nature with all of their force:*
> *Water, Fire, Air, and Earth! I call upon the power of water!*

7. Pick up your crystal or wand and chant:

> *Clouds as black at the night,*
> *I call upon you to show your might,*
> *Come here and bring your storm.*
> *Beneath clouds formed, more water is born.*
> *Show your strength and your thunder.*
> *I invoke the storm, the Earth to cover.*
> *So mote it be.*

CASTING A SHADOW CIRCLE

Hold your sacred dagger (athame) in your non-dominant hand and create a circle, while imagining shadows of creatures scratching and clawing at you. Imagine the dark shadowy creatures whirling around you and starting to create pressure upon your body, as their energies compress together and become colder. Feel the pressure and icy coldness from the Abyss of whence they came circling around you, darting against your skin. As they close in against your body, all of the outside is blocked by darkness. Switch your sacred dagger to your dominant hand. This is your shadow circle. Beware of the power of the energies you have created. Speak aloud your intent. Cast your spell and then close the circle by cutting it with your dagger. Once you establish a trusting relationship with the shadows you can ask for their ultimate protection.

SUMMONING SUCCUBAE'S LAMENT

The spell has to be cast on a new moon.

Materials

- New Moon
- White chalk
- 5 Black candles
- 5 Obsidian crystals
- Black Salt

Steps

1. Using white chalk, create a sacred pentagram. Nothing can cross the line once drawn.
2. Outside the line of chalk, lay black salt in a circle around the pentagram
3. Place the five black candles inside of the pentagram at equal distance from each other.
4. Outside the pentagram, lay five protective black obsidian crystals around you.
5. Meditate and imagine the pentagram separating you from everything outside the circle.
6. Light the candles.

7. Lay your body within the pentagram with your legs apart and your arms straight out and summon the succubus.
8. Imagine feeling her energy and forming a shadow you can interact with.

INVOCATION OF LYSSA

Lyssa is known to govern anger and rage and is referred to as the Goddess of Rage. It is very important to get to know Lyssa and familiarize yourself with her energy before asking her for her help. Here are the steps for invoking Lyssa and asking her to help you in how to build your rage.

Steps

1. Using white chalk, draw three large pentagrams on the ground with one on top and two next to each other beneath it, in the shape of a triangle.
2. Stand in the center of the triangle of pentagrams.
3. Meditate on why you feel anger and when the feeling of rage comes over you, summon Lyssa, chanting:

> *Oh powerful Goddess Lyssa, your mother is the Nobel Nyx,*
> *I ask of you for guidance and help as I am a child of the darkness, like you.*
> *Rage has been gathered within my heart and I ask your help in releasing it upon those who wish to harm me. I ask of you to teach me your artistic manifestations of rage and guide me in my magic endeavors. If I am linked to you, I can accomplish anything!*

4. You will know you have connected with Lyssa if you feel her presence and energy. If you don't, meditate more on your rage and try again.

5. Once you have established a relationship with Lyssa, nourish it with offerings and conversation regularly to keep her favor.

LIAR'S LAMENTATION SPELL

Materials

- 4 Quarters
- 1 Onion
- 1 Cup of wine

Steps

1. Carve the liar's name on the onion.
2. Speak aloud your intention and ask the earth for help.
3. Start ripping the onion layer by layer. By doing so, you are symbolically tearing away the phony fronts of the liar that they use for deception.
4. Keep tearing until you have exposed the core of the onion, which is also the core of the liar.
5. Throw the onion outside where it can rot away. The liar's deception will rot with it.
6. Leave the 4 nickels on the ground as an offering to the earth.

A SEDUCTION SPELL

This is a very strong seduction spell that will have the person you cast it upon unable to sleep without thinking of you. It will consume them until you are together. It can also bring back a lost love you desire.

Materials

- 13 Black candles (small)
- 1 Chicken heart
- Photo or item belonging to the person with whom you are casting the spell
- Parchment paper and pencil
- Twine

Steps

1. Lay the parchment paper down flat in front of you.
2. In pencil write the following:

> *Great Gods of the rushing rivers*
> *Rein your power down on (the person's name).*
> *Break them until they fall so deeply for me*
> *and if I choose so, for an eternity.*
> *So mote it be.*

3. Create a sacred circle around the paper with the black candles.

4. Standing over and looking down on your written passage, place the item belonging to that person in the center.

5. Light one candle at a time and place of drop of each one's wax on the item, focusing intensely on your intention.

6. Place the chicken heart on top of the wax drippings.

7. Blow out each candle chanting:

> *As it should be, as it is.*

8. Bury the package by a tree.

9. On the next full moon, return to the tree with the 13 candles.

10. Make a circle with the candles over the burial site.

11. Light them and let them burn all the way down while you meditate on the spell.

12. Close the circle and clean up the area.

"TATTERED HEARTS" SPELL PART I

This spell is cast to end a relationship, but Tattered Hearts Part II Spell is cast to mend one of the hearts from the ended relationship as a result of Part I.

Materials

- 2 Pieces of Heart Shaped Material. You can draw a heart on some spare fabric and cut it out.
- Needle and thread
- Sharpie
- 2 Candles, 1 black, 1 red.

Steps

1. With your sharpie, write the name of the couple, one on each heart.
2. Sew the hearts, with just a few stitches, together.
3. Light the candles and chant:

> *What together is now,*
> *Is soon torn apart.*
> *Stars fade with time.*
> *The couple departs.*
> *So mote it be.*

4. Rip the hearts apart.

5. Blow out the candle to finish this spell.

"TATTERED HEARTS" SPELL PART II

This is the second part of the spell. It will bring you the person to whom you are attracted. Hopefully, you were positive about your feelings before you cast Part I.

Steps

1. Prepare a bowl of water from the sea.
2. Cast a sacred circle.
3. Take the heart of the person you want to be with from the two hearts in Part I and place it in the bowl.
4. Chant:

> ***I know your heart is broken;***
> ***I am here to ease your pain.***
> ***With darkness gone, then I come along,***
> ***The end was not in vain.***
> ***So mote it be.***

5. Take the heart out of the sea water and put it somewhere to air dry.

6. The spell will be in effect unless you decide to break the spell by destroying the heart.

7. If that happens, burn the heart in your cauldron with the flame of a white candle.

CARMAN'S HEX

This hex came from an old woman from Ireland. She said it is a simple hex that can be used in any spell or ritual. It sounds like a nursery rhyme, with a hex at the end.

> *"Tables, knives, chairs, forks*
> *Cups, bottles, tankards, and corks,*
> *Beds, bottles, dishes, and keg,*
> *Pudding, milk, bacon, and eggs*
> *All of the sheets on the bed*
> *The spices in cupboards and the baked bread*
> *Every provision on the shelf,*
> *All you'll have left is the house itself!"*
> **Binding by Fear**

Materials

- Black Candle
- Lighter
- Black thread
- Photo of target or write their full name on a piece of paper
- Jar

Steps

1. Prepare your altar.
2. Light the black candle.
3. Tightly tie up the picture with the black thread, so you cannot see any of the face.
4. Chant:

> *Whether far or near,*
> *You will feel the fear,*

> *You caused it you know,*
> *Deservedly so.*
> *I have the key.*
> *So mote it be.*

5. Drip the black wax over the tied-up bundle until it touches on all sides.

6. Put the wax covered bundle in the jar.

7. Hide the jar at nighttime.

SPELL TO BIND A BULLY

Before we even start discussing this spell, you must make sure you are binding a bully! The whole reason for casting a binding spell is to "bind someone's powers to prevent them from doing harm." The key point here is that if you use a binding spell only for protection and justice, you are safe from any negative karmic backlash. The best time to cast this spell is during a waning moon.

Materials

- Piece of paper and pen
- Black sea salt (you can use white sea salt too)
- Black thread
- Black candle

Steps

1. On a piece of paper, write the name of the bully and put it in the center of your altar.

2. Light your black candle.

3. Take your sea salt and make a circle around the bully's name moving in a clockwise direction.

4. Take your black thread and tie it around the paper, crumpling it.

5. Chant:

> **(Name of the bully), I bind you.**
> **You are harmless to all other people and to the planet.**
> **Your hostility and insults are powerless.**
> **You can cause no harm from this day on.**
> **So mote it be.**

6. Repeat the chant six times.

7. Snuff out the candle.

8. Leave the knotted spell in the salt until morning.

9. Brush the salt onto another piece of paper and flush it down the toilet.

10. Throw the knotted paper and the bully's name into the flame.

SPELL FOR STOPPING HARASSMENT

Materials

- Blade or athame
- Brown candle
- Honey
- Piece of parchment paper
- Pen

Steps

1. Scribe the person's name on the back and front of the brown candle.

2. In the center of the candle use your athame to dig out a pocket of wax.

3. On a small parchment paper write:

From this day on, (target's name) speaks only nice words about me. This spell is cast. So mote it be.

4. Place one drop of honey in the middle of the parchment paper and ball it up.

5. Stick the balled-up paper in the dug-out pocket in the candle (imagine sticking it in the person's mouth).

6. Let the candle burn for 15 minutes every other night for nine nights.

7. Save some of the wax drippings.

8. Throw the candle into running water away from your home or hold it under running water for a few minutes and then throw it away in the outside garbage.

9. Scatter the wax drippings in the path of the person harassing you. If you don't have any wax drippings, use ash or black salt.

SOUR JAR

Sour jars do exactly as their name suggests. They sour a person's life or they can be used to sour a relationship that you want to break up. All you need is a jar half-filled with vinegar and ⅛ cup of mustard seeds.

Steps

1. Take a paper with your intention written on it using the person's or people's name(s).
2. Put it in the jar.
3. Add a bunch of "yucky" stuff like rusty nails, pet shedding, broken glass, a rotten egg, etc.
4. Keep the jar for one month and then bury it outside.

DISCORD AND DARKNESS SPELL

This spell becomes manifested by focusing your mind on projecting chaos, so make sure you are good and angry before starting.

Materials

- Piece of black yarn
- Salt

Steps

1. Make three knots in your black yarn, place it on your altar.

2. Circle the yarn with salt.

3. Chant:

> *Three knots to seal this hex,*
> *No sleep for you, nor any rest.*
> *Discord shows you to your fate.*
> *Knots of rage are not too late.*
> *I tied another knot, now two,*
> *To send the darkness over you.*

> *A third knot, now I bind,*
> *Spreading discord through your mind.*
> *As it is and should be.*
> *So mote it be.*

4. Hide the yarn where it cannot be disturbed, until you are ready to untie the knots and undo the spell.

BAD LUCK POTION

Drink a cup of this potion in combination with the previous Discord and Darkness Spell to eliminate the person that is troubling your life.

Ingredients

- Smoky quartz crystal
- Dark colored glass potion bottle or jar (or you can tape black paper around the bottle when finished and use a gold ink pen to mark a sigil on the label.
- Bay leaf
- ⅛ teaspoon cayenne pepper
- Distilled water
- Black licorice extract

Steps

1. Place the smoky quartz crystal in the distilled water and leave under moonlight overnight to charge.

2. Add the rest of the ingredients.

3. Remove the crystal and bury it in black soil.

4. Store your potion in a cool dry place or in the refrigerator.

"RING OF POWER" ENCHANTMENT

Materials

- Rock salt
- Black obsidian crystal ring
- Goblet with blessed water

Steps

1. Sprinkle rock salt into the goblet of blessed water.

2. Place your goblet in the center of your altar.

3. Put the ring into the goblet.

4. Chant:

> ***I am granted the power in my hands***
> ***From Sea, Air, Fire, and Land.***
> ***The Goddess and Elements give power to me,***
> ***With this spell, more powerful I'll be.***
> ***So mote it be.***

5. After three hours, remove the ring and put it on a finger of your dominant hand.

6. Wear the ring for nine days without letting anyone touch it.

7. Repeat the spell every day for nine days while rubbing the crystal.

8. Feel and acknowledge the powerful feelings entering your body.

9. Give thanks to the elements and goddess with an offering on your altar.

EFFIGY POPPET CURSE

Materials

- Black fabric
- Paper and pen
- Black thread and needle
- Black candle
- Graveyard dirt
- Tobacco
- Cayenne Pepper
- Black Salt
- Black obsidian crystal

Steps

1. Do this by the light of a black candle.
2. Write your target's name on a piece of paper.
3. Cut your poppet out of the fabric; cut two matching pieces.
4. Sew it together leaving the top open for stuffing.
5. Place all of your ingredients into the poppet and sew closed.
6. Carry your poppet and black candle to your altar and whisper your hex in its ear:

    Whatever happens to this poppet, you will feel too.
    "Person's name" is this poppet, this poppet is you.
    My whisper to this poppet, you will know true.
    As you are this poppet and this poppet is you.
    So mote it be.

"NIGHTMARE JAR" SPELL

Materials

- 1 small jar with top
- Black sharpie
- Black candle
- Black salt
- Black yarn (8 inches)
- Lock of hair from the target you want to protect or your own
- 10 Rusty nails
- 10 Pieces of broken glass
- Mint leaves
- Bay leaves

Steps

1. Light your candle.
2. Place the lock of hair into the jar.
3. Place nails and broken glass in the jar.
4. Add the herbs.
5. Add ½ of your black salt imagining it sucking the negative energy from your target into the darkness to remain forever. Picture a black hole with the nightmares speeding into it.
6. Pour in the rest of your salt.
7. Put 20 drops of candle wax in the jar.
8. Write the name of the target on a piece of white paper with the sharpie.
9. Put it into the jar.
10. Add 10 drops of candle wax on top of the name of the person.
11. Seal the jar.
12. Place the jar under the moonlight for charging.

13. Keep the jar in a window for continuous charging to banish the nightmares.

"BANISHING YOUR EX" HEX

Sometimes exes just won't go away and will continue to make our lives miserable. If you have tried everything known to mankind to get rid of your ex, this is your next step. Make sure you want to be rid of this person for good and that you are not just temporarily angry.

Materials

- Picture of your ex
- Pen
- Paper
- Black candle
- White candle
- Sage
- Abalone shell

Steps

1. Open all of the windows and turn on any fans in the house.

2. Light the white candle.

3. Start burning your sage and chanting while walking around and cleansing your entire house, waving in a clockwise direction. Cover every corner, every window, and every door, repeating the chant:

> ***I purge myself of (ex's name) and all of their negativity.***
> ***So mote it be.***

4. As you watch the smoke fly out of the windows, imagine the smoke taking your ex with it.

5. Write your ex's name on the piece of paper.

6. Imagine your life with your ex no longer in it.

7. Burn the paper.

8. As quickly as it burns, take the ashes outside and toss them to the wind.

"YOU'RE SO VAIN AND INSANE" HEX

This spell is for a person who is so vain they don't even think about anyone else. Once cast, they will lose their vanity when they look in the mirror.

Materials

- Item belonging to target
- Black marker
- Black candle
- Flammable poppet
- Fireproof bowl or cauldron

Steps

1. Go outdoors.

2. Take the item belonging to your target.

3. Write the target's name on the poppet with the black marker.

4. Put the poppet in the cauldron and ignite it and chant:

> *(Target's name), for all to see,*
> *Begone your feelings of vanity.*
> *You will see yourself like others do.*

Begone all vanity now from you.
So mote it be.

BUSINESS BUTCHER CURSE

1. Relax and take some time to meditate on the nasty workings of the business you are going to curse.
2. Draw a red circle on a piece of paper.
3. Focus on a specific issue that draws you in and ask yourself "who or what is the cause for this situation?"
4. You will most likely come to a conclusion about which entity or entities are causing you or yours harm or distress.
5. Write the name of the business in the middle of the red circle.
6. Focus your intention on how much better things will be without the organization.
7. Either use tape or a glue stick and stick it somewhere on the building of the business where it cannot be seen.
8. Feel good that you have now conducted your first tactical magic spell!

POPPET CURSE OF SLIGHT PAIN

This spell is for that person you wish you could just slap or punch because of all the pain they've caused you. Fortunately, with this spell, you can do just that.

Materials

- Poppet (use the method from the earlier poppet spell or carve a person's name in a bar of soap)

STEPS

1. Hold your poppet in your dominant hand and slowly grip it tighter. After focusing on your rage toward the target, drop it on the floor.
2. Your poppet is now charged and ready to do magic
3. You can now punch it or thump it on the arm.
4. The stronger your intention, the more harm that can be inflicted.

"AGONY OF ACNE" CURSE

Materials

- A small item with your target's DNA on it
- Grime and dirt
- 1 small vile
- 1 Black Candle
- 1 Red Candle

Steps

1. Put the DNA in the vile.
2. Put the grime and dirt in the vile.
3. Drip wax from both candles in the vile.
4. Bury the vile in your target's yard.

"EVIL EYE" ENCHANTMENT

The belief in the evil eye curse goes back to cave drawings from over 10,000 years ago that were discovered in Spain. It is believed that a person will cast an evil eye with a certain glare in their eyes to someone who is vain, bragging about their wealth, showing no respect for others, or gossiping. Wearing a glass evil eye symbol will reflect back any malicious intent onto the caster. The curse can cause a number of ailments that can range from small annoyances to major catastrophes. The ritual to cast off or remove the curse of the evil eye is through releasing the negative vibrations instilled in the curse. The evil eye is composed of black energy that affects a person's mental, emotional, and spiritual realms.

Steps to Ward Off the Evil Eye

1. Wearing jewelry depicting the evil eye will protect you from the curse and reflect it back on the person who cast it.
2. Write down on a piece of paper "buri nazar wale tera muh kala" ("O evil-eyed one, may your face turn black") and carry it in your wallet.
3. Using wall hangings of the evil eye will protect you and your home.
4. Sweep a raw egg over your body or the body of the person cursed. Break the egg into a glass of blessed water and put it under the head of the bed of the cursed person.
5. Phallic charms to ward off the evil have been practiced for centuries.

5

RUNE CASTING & DIVINATION

SOME OF THE WICCAN PRACTITIONERS' DIVINATION IS ACHIEVED by casting runes. Similar to Tarot card readings, casting runes is not about predicting the future or fortune-telling, so to speak. Rather, it is an enlightenment tool that works in conjunction with your subconscious to help with problem-solving and possible outcomes. While sometimes you may come across obscure meanings, most people have learned to be specific with their questions and base them on their current circumstances. Rune casting has been around since ancient Roman times and appears again in the Norse Sagas and Eddas. While you can buy runes that are pre-made, creating your own puts more of your own energy into them.

The term for making your own runes is "risting." Historically, runes were made from nut-bearing trees or pine, hazel, oak, or cedar. You can burn, carve, or paint the symbols on your runes. Some people paint stones and top them with acrylic to keep the symbols from rubbing off with use. Risting runes is part of their magical properties and should only be done when you achieve enough knowledge and proper preparation. Furthermore, using a white colored cloth to cast your runes upon makes it easier for you to cast them. However, some people prefer to cast runes on the ground. Keep runes stored in a sacred pouch or box when you are not using them.

TIWAZ (TYR)

TIWAX is the rune of justice and balance. It is ruled by higher rationality and is the rune of self-sacrifice to the best interest of others and society as a whole. It is associated with fairness, keeping the peace, and the rule of law.

Letter in the alphabet: 23

Color: Bright red

Element: Air

Tree: Oak

Herb: Sage

Crystals: Garnet, jasper, topaz, citrine, ruby, and bloodstone

Animals: Hawk, owl, bear, falcon, and hound

Energy: Sacrifice, appropriate decision making, supreme order, honor, warrior, and righteousness.

Magical Use: Loyalty, analysis, honesty, rationality, faith, victory, self-sacrifice and over-sacrifice.

Divinations: honesty, faith, loyalty, justice, rationality, self-sacrifice, analysis, victory OR defeat, injustice, overly sacrificing and tyranny.

BERKANO (BIRCH GODDESS)

The Birch Goddess or BERKANO rune is all about renewal and rebirth. It governs gardening and is known as the Earth Mother and the rune of becoming. Its energy is associated with plant life, trees, and female fertility. The Birch Goddess is healing and connected to the womb and raising children.

Letter in the alphabet: 18

Color: Dark green

Element: Earth

Tree: Birch

Herb: Lady's mantle

Crystals: All

Animals: All

Energy: Wisdom, silence, dependence, and safety

Magical Uses: Metabolism and excretion, harmony, strengthens powers of secrecy, openness, creativity, and dance.

Divinations: Sanctuary, changes in life, becoming, confidence, shelter, secrets, birth OR sterility, insecurity, and deceit.

EHWAZ (HORSE)

EHWAZ or Horse is the rune of trust and teamwork, which refers to two entities working together toward the same goal. It is also the rune of sexuality.

Letter in the alphabet: 19

Color: Red

Element: Earth

Tree: Yew

Crystal: Topaz

Herb: Ragwort

Animal: Horse

Energy: Cooperation and trust, friendship, and animals.

Magical uses: An entity who is within you and with you in all of your incarnations is known as The Fetch. EHWAS activates your Fetch. Also known as the horse, this rune helps you bond with all animals (horse whisperer), allowing you to uncover deceit quickly.

Divinations: Marriage and teamwork, a friend, loyalty, harmony, trust OR disharmony, mistrust, nightmares, an enemy, indecision, and betrayal.

MANNAZ (MANKIND)

MANNAZ is the rune of mind, learning, and memory. It is the humanitarian rune. Invoking MANNAZ provides you with entry into humanity and Earth's collective unconscious.

Letter of the alphabet: 20

Color: Red

Element: Air

Tree: Holly

Crystal: Garnet

Herb: Madder

Animal: Man

Energy: Transformation from past lives, dreams, and the unconscious

Magical Uses: Self-actualization, raises intelligence, higher self-awareness, mental powers and memory (perfect if you need to pass a test), unlocks the mind's eye (the third eye), acknowledgment of the divine structure in all beings, spiritual and mental potential.

Divinations: Intelligence, social order, sustainability, awareness, driving influence, OR bigotry, elitism, blindness, depression, arrogance, and mortality.

LAGUZ (WATER)

The LAGUZ rune is associated with hidden powers, change, and the sea. This rune refers to your intuition powers, and the listening skills necessary to live a life of complete freedom.

Letter of the alphabet: 21

Colors: Orange, Blue, Dark green

Element: Water

Tree: Willow

Crystal: Pearl

Herb: Amaranth

Animal: Otter and seal

Energy: The spirit of the sea, the astral plane, unity in love, life energy, evolution, and the origin of life

Magical uses: Change, empathy, increased energy, dreams, mystery, collective unconscious, and the ability to adapt. Primal fears and insecurities.

Divinations: Memory, dreams, vitality of the sea, fantasy, growth, circular motion, OR depression, emotional blackmail, withering, avoidance, lack of morality, poison, manipulation, and toxicity.

INGWAZ OR INGUZ (SEED)

The INGWAZ OR INGUZ has great power and symbolizes a new path in your life, or a new life. It will shed enough strength to reach a resolution, which results in a fresh start. INGUZ governs transformational power in ritual use and how to center your thoughts and energy through passive meditation .

Letter of the alphabet: 22

Colors: Gold, orange, yellow, green

Elements: Water and earth

Tree: Willow

Crystal: Amber

Herb: Self-heal

Animal: Boar

Energy: Mysteries of the male, earth-god, process of gestation, energy storage

Magical uses: Inner-child, personal growth, wholeness, powers of suggestion.

Divinations: Personal growth or immaturity, self-care OR frivolity, gestation or impotence, expectation or inability to change.

DAGAZ (DAWN)

The DAGAZ rune, meaning Dawn, governs the ability to become invisible and receive the gift of mystical inspiration. It has the ability to transform things into their opposite state as it integrates the male and female into one being who feels complete.

Letter of the Alphabet: 14

Colors: Blue, light blue, yellow, orange, and red

Element: Fire

Tree: Spruce

Crystal: Peridot and diamond

Herb: Mullein

Animal: Raven, wolf, eagle, and bear

Energy: Represents the light at dawn and at dusk, synthesis, unity, transmutation, and non-dual reality

Magical uses: Self-esteem, truth, perseverance, hospitality, loyalty, honor, industriousness, courage, truth, and honor.

Divinations: Hope and happiness, awareness, paradigm shift, the ideal, and awakening OR insomnia, hopelessness, catastrophic change.

RAIDHO (RIDING)

RAIDHO symbolizes life's journey and is connected to the inner-self and the daylight. It will take you down the right path with nobility and merit.

Letter of the Alphabet: 5

Colors: Bright red, blue, and dusty brown

Element: Air

Tree: Oak

Crystal: Chrysoprase

Herb: Mugwort

Animal: Pack animals and horse

Energy: Rhythm active presence, and cosmic cyclical law

Magical Uses: Transportation, adventure, counsel, moral compass, integrity, rituals, initiative, nobility, control of oneself, celestial procession, and the right action.

Divinations: Justice, journey, action, sound advice, ordered growth, OR stasis, irrationality, restlessness, crisis, rigidity, wrongful imprisonment, hypocrisy, and control freak.

KENAZ (TORCH)

KENAZ symbolizes intellect, knowledge, mastery of fire, creation, and cremation. It governs ability, magic, and art.

Letter of the Alphabet: 6

Colors: Red, white, pink, blue, grey, red-golds, brown, and yellow.

Element: Fire

Tree: Pine

Crystal: Bloodstone

Herb: Cowslip

Animal: Dragon

Energy: Learning-teaching dynamic, transformation, and illumination

Magical Uses: Skills, creativity, craftsmanship, intuition, quest for truth, intellect and knowledge, playfulness, study, opportunity, occult female secrecy, cunning.

Divinations: Craft, offspring, ability, transformation, OR decay, ignorance, elitism, breakup, disease, lacking creativity, and inability.

GEBO (GIFT)

Each decision made in life requires an acceptance with a simultaneous release or sacrifice. It tells you that something good is coming your way that might be money or it might be love.

Letter of the Alphabet: 7

Colors: Rose and deep blue

Element: Air

Tree: Elm and ash

Crystal: Opal

Herb: Eucalyptus

Animal: Owl

Energy: Sacrifice, resolving barriers by the act of gift giving, and exchanged powers.

Magical Uses: Generosity, hospitality, obligations, contracts, dept, favors, and taking an oath.

Divinations: Gifting, sacrifice, generosity, honor, divine vision OR greed, dependence, dishonesty, moodiness, and loneliness.

WUNJO (JOY)

WUNJO surrounds the principles of ecstasy and joy, as well as inner harmony. It is about family, bonding, shared identity, and cooperation. It symbolizes our inner-child and makes for a happy couple.

Letter of the Alphabet: 8

Colors: Indigo, blue, yellow, light blue, light green

Element: Earth

Tree: Ash

Crystal: Diamond

Herb: Flax

Animal: Wolf

Energy: Fellowship, friendship, harmony, effortlessness, wishing, and harmony of like forces

Magical Uses: Shared identity, optimism, contentment, family, parties, friendship, goal achievement, enlightenment, and hope.

Divinations: Accomplishment, harmony, prosperity, fellowship OR strife, betrayal, stupidity, alienation, and deception.

HAGALAZ (HAIL)

HAGALAZ or Hail is a powerful rune, symbolizing spiritual fulfillment and protection. It is associated with your dreams and emotions as a cleansing agent. HAGALAZ governs regression, acceptance, and psychoanalysis.

Letter of the Alphabet: 9

Colors: Indigo, dark brownish

green, grey, black and bright green.

Elements: Earth and water

Tree: Ash

Crystal: Onyx

Herb: Lily-of-the-Valley

Animal: Falcon, owl, whale, wolf, eagle, hawk, vulture, and dolphin

Energy: Superhuman powers, violent natural forces, seed forming, chaos, and the ability to confront someone objectively

Magical Uses: Transformation, confrontation, banishing spells for protection, awakening the subconscious of others through brutal honesty.

Divinations: Changes for the long run goals, crisis management, inner harmony, completion, and corrections; OR crisis, stagnation, property loss, blame, stuck in the past, victimization, catastrophe, disappointment, obsessing about the past.

NAUTHIZ (NECESSITY)

NAUTHIZ is the rune of fate, constriction, relief and vital fire. It governs acceptance, magical ability development, and overcoming distress. This rune is great energy for generating problem-solving abilities and for protecting your own needs. This is the rune for love spells.

Letter of the Alphabet: 10

Colors: Dark Red and black

Element: Fire

Tree: Beech

Crystal: Lapis lazuli

Herb: Bistort

Animal: Cow

Energy: Urgency, coming forth, and necessity.

Magical Uses: Stress management, protection, hard work, chores, summoning the Sun's power, and cleansing.

Divinations: Recognition of primal truth, innovation, strength in resistance, personal growth, self-reliance, and life lessons; OR distress, worry, cowardice, guilt, drudgery, toil, warnings and unfulfilled needs.

ISA (ICE)

ISA is the rune of being in a frozen or static state and of concentration. It governs the ego and a state of stillness. It is associated with self-mastery. From ISA we learn that death is part of life.

Letter of the Alphabet: 10

Colors: Black, white, pale and bright blue

Element: Water

Tree: Alder

Crystal: Cat's eye

Herb: Henbane

Animal: Polar bear

Energy: Frozen, stillness, stasis, and contraction

Magical Uses: Protection, freezes negative forces from entering your space, power over unwanted outbursts, defense and destruction.

Divinations: Self-control, unity, self-care OR dullness, psychopathy, egomania, immobility, and blindness.

ANSUZ (SPEECH)

ANSUZ or the speech rune governs the cognitive senses and speech. It will mentally inspire you. ANSUZ is associated with a baby's first breath and the last breath before death. ANSUZ transmits magical powers from generation to generation, giving way to the truth that there is no divide between us and the universe.

Letter of the Alphabet: 4

Colors: Sky blue, grey, and dark blue.

Element: Air

Tree: Ash

Crystal: Emerald

Herb: Fly Agaric

Animal: Raven and wolf

Energy: Communication, answers, sovereign ancestral god, spirit, and exploration

Magical Uses: Communion, listening, inspiration, and stability.

Divinations: Intellect, open communication, power in words, transformation, OR bad advice, misunderstandings, delusions, and being easily manipulated.

THURISAZ (THORN)

THURISAZ is symbolic of Thor's hammer. It is associated with the consciousness of the Warrior and matters requiring wisdom with force. It is about being the ultimate force in fighting for freedom for all human beings. If you want to combat blockages in your spirit, mind and body, THURISAZ is the rune to cast.

Letter of the Alphabet: 3

Colors: Dark and bright red, white, grey, and purple

Elements: Fire and water

Tree: Thorn and oak

Crystal: Sapphire

Herb: House Leek

Animal: Raven, crow, and wolf

Energy: Chaos, empowerment, resistance breaker, violent storms, forces of defense, and enthusiasm

Magical Uses: Struggles with your unconsciousness, enthusiasm, sexual prowess, masculinity, and creating boundaries.

Divinations: Direct force, conflict resolution, reactive force, regeneration, OR betrayal, disease, combative violence, annoyance, dullness, and defenselessness.

OTHALA (HOMELAND)

OTHALA (ODAL), or the rune of the homeland, governs over fences. It governs over ancestral spiritual powers, property, and divine inheritance. It helps us figure out our societal role. If you're looking for some wise advice, OTHALA is the place to ask for it.

Letter of the Alphabet: 23

Colors: Red, brown, dark yellow,

Elements: Earth

Tree: Hawthorn

Crystal: Ruby

Herb: Clover

Animal: Beaver

Energy: Paradise, inheritance, ancestral spiritual powers, utopia, and heaven on earth

Magical Uses: Collects knowledge and powers from generations past, wealth of property, deserved inheritance from ancestors, comprehension of global unity, safety, security, royalty, and protection.

Divinations: Freedom, prosperity, estate or home, group order, productive interactions OR homelessness, slavery, xenophobia, totalitarianism, lack of order, genocide, and poverty.

JERA (YEAR)

JERA or the Year rune represents the union between heaven and earth, the life cycle, the sun's cycle, and the eternal return. It governs peace in the heart and on land, naturally ordered actions, and harvest. It is associated with planning for the future. Like the sleep cycle, dawn to dusk, JERA signifies the heartbeat and the breath.

Letter of the Alphabet: 12

Colors: Red gold, black, brown, green, and light blue

Elements: Earth

Tree: Oak

Crystal: Cornelian

Herb: Rosemary

Animal: Firefly

Energy: Orbits, biorhythms, good harvest, good effort, and progress

Magical Uses: Creativity, prosperity, peace, fertility, harmony, and plenty. Invoking the power of the cycles and times, brings to you the acknowledgement of the universe's cyclic nature. Brings intention into manifestations and initiates a lasting but gradual change in the flow of life.

Divinations: Plenty, good timing, being rewarded from positive action, peace OR conflict, bad timing, repetition, poverty, and regression.

EIHWAZ OR IHWAZ (YEW TREE)

EIHWAZ or IHWAZ, the rune of the Yew Tree and of the secrets of life and death. This rune suggests the opportunities that come when you risk a different path. It is usually a sign of waiting and tells you to keep looking towards the future.

Letter of the Alphabet: 13

Colors: Red gold, black, brown, green, and light blue

Elements: Earth

Tree: Yew

Crystal: Topaz

Herb: Mandrake

Animal: Eagle, spider, eel, lizard, hound, horse, wolf, raven, serpent, dragon, jaguar, dolphin, salmon, butterfly, dragonfly, kingfish, and moth

Energy: Encoding, balancing the chakra system, and secrecy

Magical Uses: Allows you the wisdom of the chakras, and World Tree (Yggdrasil), will help you to develop your spiritual endurance, communication between different realities, and your ability to gain the initiative for any endeavor.

Divinations: In the direction of Enlightenment, initiation, protection, endurance OR weakness, destruction, confusion, dissatisfaction, and death.

PERTHRO (UNKNOWN)

PERTHRO's true meaning is unknown, but is thought to be a rune of favorable circumstances. It is associated with the Great Goddess and therefore reflects timelessness, magical transformation, and spiritual regeneration. This rune provides you with a direction, but gives you the free will to make the right choice. It symbolizes actions and reactions and the fundamental mysteries of the universe.

Letter of the Alphabet: 14

Colors: Black, green and silver

Elements: Water

Tree: Beech

Crystal: Aquamarine

Herb: Aconite

Animal: Water moccasin, hound, falcon, hawk, and wolf

Energy: Nothingness, the unmanifested, luck and evolutionary forces

Magical Uses: Manipulate cause and effect, higher probability of luck, creates favorable circumstances, gambling, guessing, chance, and divination.

Divinations: Good luck, joy, fellowship, evolution, knowledge, OR addictions, delusions, unknowability, stagnation, and loneliness.

ALGIZ (LIFE)

ALGIZ is the rune of life, independence, faith, and autonomy. It will provide you with courage when facing fear. However, it does not banish fear, in case fear is spawned as a warning. It gives you the insight you need to make good judgments.

Letter of the Alphabet: 15

Colors: Black, silver, and green

Elements: Air

Tree: Yew

Crystal: Amethyst

Herb: Angelica

Animal: Deer and elk

Energy: The divine plane, teaching and protection, Valkyries from the battlefield to Valhalla

Magical Uses: Strengthens your life force through courageous acts and allows you to understand things which are not human. Religious and mystical communications with other universes, defense and protection. Banishes the fear of death. Spirituality and safety.

Divinations: Awakening higher awareness, connection with the Goddesses, higher life, protection, OR loss of the link to the divine, fear, hidden danger, and dissipation by divine powers.

SOWILO (SUN)

SOWILO or the sun rune is the force that runs counter to the rune ISA. It governs the force of fire in the mental and physical world and promotes optimism, persistence, dedication, and invigoration in all endeavors. It will guard you against the hurtful opinions of others so your heart will stay focused on your intentions.

Letter of the Alphabet: 16

Colors: Gold, blue, silver, white, yellow, and green

Elements: Fire

Tree: Juniper

Crystal: Ruby

Herb: Hedge wolf

Animal: Rooster

Energy: Strengthens chakras, life-giving force, motivation, sun-wheel, and action

Magical Uses: Transformation of thoughts into action, activates your highest value system, wellness, will guide your way to enlightenment, increase your psychic abilities, success driven by self.

Divinations: Hope, faith, purpose in life, honor, success, and goals, OR gullibility, no goals, poor advice, and false success.

FEHU (CATTLE)

The Fehu or cattle rune symbolizes two cow's horns or two branches of a tree. Historically, families with many cattle were considered wealthy. Cattle was used in the past in the same fashion as money is used today. If you cast the FEHU rune, success and wealth will be arriving soon. The Fehu rune carries with it a cautionary warning. That is to use these earnings on something permanent or solid once they come. It will remind you how fast money can slip through your fingers, if you don't spend it carefully. It is associated with your goals and dreams. It may be indicating that you have debts piling up and you should be on the road to satisfying them immediately.

When inverted, Fehu references a dark side of wealth. It can symbolize corruption and can also be reminding you to be careful with your money and properties, rather than letting them control you. Money, like all things, can be used for both good and evil. It carries with it both negativity and positivity. As such, Fehu inverted references to the dark side of money.

Letter of the alphabet: 2

Color: Red

Elements: Fire and earth

Tree: Elder

Crystal: Moss Agate

Herb: Nettle

Animal: Cow

Energy: Sustainability, circulation, expansive energy

Magical Uses: Social success, travel, wealth, fresh beginnings, generosity, foresight, power, reputation, sexual energy, fertile harvest, crisis management, luck, control, increased psychic strength, and breaking the spirit of an adversary.

Divinations: Money, foresight, fresh beginnings, travel, social success; OR failure, poverty, greed, endings, and atrophy.

URUZ (AUROCHS)

URUZ or Aurochs is a powerful rune of the unconscious, which is shaping your energies that need guided wisdom as they manifest. It is a cautionary rune, reminding you that untamed creative powers can be dangerous. This is a reality evident in our civilization's use of modern technology. It is the practitioner's practiced methods and skill level that will control the energy untethered from this rune. URUZ is associated with assertiveness, independence, and one's own territory.

Letter of the alphabet: 2

Color: Dark Green

Tree: Birch

Crystal: Carbuncle

Herb: Sphagnum Moss

Animal: Cow

Elements: Fire

Energy: Healing, raw primal power, organic structuring, vital forces, manifestation, survival, and quintessential patterning

Magical Uses: Self-care, personal space, courage, rites of passage, health and wellness, freedom, creativity, inspiration, independence, and freedom.

Divinations: Vitality, pattern, tenacity, strength, luck, constancy, practical knowledge, understanding, OR inconstancy, ignorance, weakness, insensitivity, misdirected rage, sickness, and brutality.

THREE NORNS METHOD

The Three Norns Method in Norse mythology is named after the three goddesses of fate. It requires picking three runes in exactly the same way as you do for the one-rune method. Place the three runes side by side (see diagram above) and read them in the order they were drawn. The reading is specific to the past, present, and future and is read from right to left.

Position 1: URD placement: reveals situations in the past that are directly related to the present and are setting the groundwork for the future.

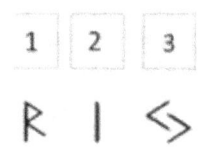

Position 2. Verdandi placement: reveals present situations and will point out any decisions that you are going to have to make very soon.

Position 3. Skuld placement: reveals a veiled future, with parts unknown. It may show you the outcome of a present dilemma or provide you with a potential future scenario that depends on your choices in life.

SCRYING

Historically, scrying has been characterized by the image of a fortune teller peering into her crystal ball. This has been used a lot in a negative way. However, scrying, like all arcane practices, is not about telling fortunes or "seeing your future." The future can only be theorized based on the information you have at the present moment. The word "scrying" is rooted in the Old English word "descry" which means to reveal or to "dimly make out." Hence, scrying references what is unseen by using our innate second sight. Our "second sight" is our ability to see aspects that usually cannot be distinguished through our five senses. Once the technique is understood, you will be able to connect to your unconscious mind. Therefore, it can be a powerful way to understand yourself. If you are having a hard time finding direction, purpose, and meaning in your life, scrying is a beautiful and amazing way to connect with your goals, dreams, and essential needs.

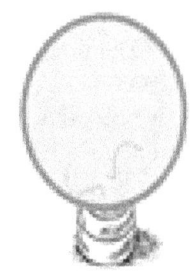

Scrying is usually performed by using a crystal ball, mirror, water, or another reflective surface. However, it is important to note that there are many other techniques. The other common techniques are:

1. Wax: The practitioner drips wax onto the surface of water. The scryer then analyzes and interprets the words or images created from the wax that has dried on the surface of the water.
2. Mirror: This is a very well-known scrying technique. Also known as catoptromancy, this method is conducted by putting yourself in a relaxed state,

further relaxing your eyes, and gazing into a mirror. It doesn't take long for scenes and images to emerge.
3. Water: Using the same technique as with mirror scrying, only gazing into a pool or body of water. Some scryers may drop a pebble into the water to read the ripples that are created.
4. Cloud: Cloud gazing is a technique whereby you observe and analyze the shapes formed by clouds. This is a special form of information gathering.
5. Oil: This is done by rubbing oil on your body, pouring some into a dish, or coating a plate or cup with oil. The scryer then pays attention to the way the light is reflected off of the oiled object for interpretation.
6. Fire: This is the oldest form of scrying and is accomplished by experiencing visions while staring into fiery flames. You can do this with an oil lamp or candle, but bonfires are magically powered for this technique.
7. Crystal: This is the crystal ball technique. Many different types of crystals are used to create magical and beautiful globes for effective readings of special meaning.
8. Smoke: Watching smoke rising from a fire creates ethereal images that provide you with spiritual information.
9. Eye: This is the most unusual! Also referred to as soul gazing, this scrying technique involves staring deeply into the eyes of a person and interpreting the reflections you see.

WATER SCRYING METHOD

Here is a water lesson for your enjoyment and to give you a starting point if you don't already have one. You're welcome to copy this technique or create your own. Also, don't feel restricted to this type of water scrying, especially if you don't feel drawn to it. Practice with the variety of techniques for scrying I described above.

Materials

- 1 Black bowl
- Moon water or blessed water (you can use purified water or collect rainwater; even better)
- 2 Black candles
- Lighter
- Clear quartz crystal
- Table
- Sage bundle or incense

Steps

1. Dark bowls help you to focus better. Fill your bowl with one of the water recipes or use bottled water.
2. Prepare your sacred space. You can be inside or outside, but you want to be in the dark. Smudge the area.
3. Place your clear quartz crystal in the center of the bowl. Clear quartz balances and amplifies your intentions. Make sure to center your crystal because it will be the focal point for your eyes.
4. Place your candles on each side of your bowl and light them.
5. Enter your meditation and transform yourself into a trance-like state. When you are in a trance, your state of consciousness is altered. Just about every culture in the world has trance rituals; some involve chanting, fasting, beating a drum, and dancing. I personally always do deep breathing exercises.
6. Once you have entered your trance, begin to gaze into

the bowl. You will know when you're ready because, in an altered state, you will feel connected, peaceful, alert, focused, and expanded. If you don't feel these emotions, take more time.

7. Most of all, relax your eyes and focus on your crystal. Water scrying can take practice to master, so be patient.
8. With your intention strong in your mind, let your eyes and your entire face relax and breathe deeply.
9. You can allow your vision to soften as images may start to come and go. Don't try to make them stay. Allow them to flow, coming and going freely, while feeling their sensations. You want to passively observe the images. This takes practice.
10. After a moment or two, you will feel your mind starting to wander. Allow this to happen. Be sure to keep your eyes focused on the water.
11. It is normal for an image or a whole scene to play out before your very eyes.
12. Once you feel you have the answers, you may want to meditate on the scenes, words, or images you have experienced.
13. Ask yourself what they were attempting to reveal to you. Sometimes, it will be extremely evident, and other times, not so much. So, look out for metaphors, analogies, and symbols that may carry a meaning close to your intention.

PENDULUM DOWSING

One of the most popular divination techniques is pendulum dowsing. A pendulum (see image above) is a weighted object, symmetrical in shape, and usually crystal in composition. Some may use beads, a metal ball, their sacred trinket, or even a key.

It never is made of material that is magnetic. The pendulum works to receive and transmit information, and shifts direction differently in response to the questions. Pendulum dowsing can help you with making decisions, answer your questions as well as other magical uses:

- Identify a person's allergies and other healing purposes.
- To dispel negative vibrations and cleanse a sacred space.
- To assist you in finding your lost pet or a lost object.
- To point you in the direction of water.

HOW PENDULUM DOWSING WORKS

Pendulum dowsing taps into your sense and intuition. The pendulum functions to receive and transmit information between your spiritual advisors and guardian angels—your higher power. As it sways, the answers to your questions will come to you. "Yes" and "no" questions are the easiest to read. Dowsing actually connects your left and right sides of the brain, which are the intuitive and logical sides of you. When those two elements are connected, you can come to decisions using all of your resources, rather than only one of them. Like all forms of magic, your intentions, faith, and beliefs are necessary for competent readings. Most commonly, dowsers use clear quartz but you only need to put the keyword "pendulum dowsing" in any search engine to see hundreds of crystal species used for dowsing. Again, use what you are drawn to or spend some time researching the many beautiful properties of crystals. The crystal you choose has to be pointed or rounded on one end. Here are some steps to follow:

1. Smudge or cleanse and charge your pendulum with any of the methods discussed in this book. Sun charging, catching the sun's rays, is also a great idea.
2. Keep it in a safe place, such as a velvet pouch or a silk wrap.
3. Put all of your doubts aside and come in with an open mind.
4. Hold the string or cord of the pendulum in whichever hand feels most comfortable, between your forefinger and your thumb.
5. If the cord feels too long, wrap it around your finger. Some pendulums come with a small ring at the top that can be held.
6. Sit comfortably with the cord of your pendulum between your thumb and forefinger. Using your other hand, run down the length of the cord, bringing your hand so it is resting with the tip of the bottom of the pendulum in your palm, facing up.
7. Now the pendulum is completely still and you can gently move away your hand from its bottom.
8. It is completely normal for the pendulum to start moving.
9. Continuing to stay relaxed watch the movement of the pendulum.
10. After a few moments, give "yes" and "no" questions a go, either aloud or in your mind.
11. Be patient when waiting for your answer. At first, ask simple questions, as it takes time to create a relationship with your pendulum and know how you both interact.
12. Practice by asking your pendulum to show you "yes" and "no" responses until you come to a full understanding of the different motions.
13. Some pendulums, when answering "yes" swing in a wide circular motion that can change with time. If

anyone touches your pendulum other than you, it will need to be cleansed and recharged with your unique energy.
14. As you become familiar with responses, you can gradually begin to inquire about personal decisions that you are making in your life.
15. You can also hold your pendulum over a map and ask it to find something you are searching for, such as a lost pet or connection.

THE FUTHARK RUNES

RUNE	NAME	TRANSLATION	MEANING
ᚠ	Fehu	F	Prosperity, wealth, fulfilment, cattle, gain
ᚢ	Uruz	U	Determination, wild ox, life force, strength
ᚦ	Thurisaz	Th	Thor, unexpected changes, giants, brutal force
ᚨ	Ansuz	A	Odin, communication, mouth, transferring of information
ᚱ	Raido	R	Travel, journey, introspection, movement, wagon
ᚲ	Kaunaz	C/K	Energy, positive attitude, fire, power, warmth

RUNE	NAME	TRANSLATION	MEANING
	Gebo	G	Partnership, gift, serendipitous outcome, commitment
	Wunjo	W	Lasting happiness, emotional joy, success
	Hagalaz	H	Disruption, hail, limitations, forces beyond your control
	Nauthiz	N	Hardship, patience, need, learning through hardship
	Isa	I	Ice, frustrations, putting your plans on hold

FINAL THOUGHTS

I hope you have enjoyed this detailed narrative about the world of witchcraft rituals, white, red, black, and rune magic with this step-by-step guide to spell casting, rune reading, and the many other concepts of magic that we have described. With this book of magical spells you should be able to sharpen your skills and set your intentions with techniques and methods that will nourish you and guide you to where you want to go as an experienced witch. I hope that I have added some incredible new spells to your magic repertoire. At this point, you have hopefully learned the techniques associated with white, red and black magic, runes, and divinations; how to conduct the ritual of calling quarters and candle magic. Interpreting runes will be ever so much easier to understand after reviewing the material outlined in this book. By reading this book you have hopefully learned how to cast a circle, cleanse your sacred space, what colors represent in the world of magic, how to call upon the elements, and so much more.

I have shared my skill set and in-depth understanding and education about casting spells and the Wiccan culture. Your life will be passionately transformed through enlightenment and spiritual connectedness.

The history of runes was explained to provide an interpretation guide for the beginner witch. Various rituals, spells, and methods, including poppet construction, scrying, pendulum dowsing, and others were outlined; you can incorporate them into your life on a daily basis and create a magical environment in which your spells can be manifested. Each spell described how to communicate your intentions by using your intuition to interpret findings and discover the worlds beyond our own. Natural potions and crystal magic are a huge component of practicing witchcraft and Wiccans have been doing the research on them for centuries.

Understanding the importance of dispelling myths about Hoodoo and black magic is a responsibility witches should share. The racist undertones are relevant in today's turbulent and trying times. People undeniably have associated black witches with black magic and other magical deeds trumped up in the media as harmful and dangerous. Historically, black witches have mainly been portrayed as evil and as only practicing hoodoo, voodoo, or other forms of stigmatized magic.

Hopefully, you gained a keen understanding of the importance of herbs and essential oils as integral components to magic. A spell or a potion is only as good as its ingredients. Many individuals have come to use essential oils and herbal remedies for balancing and unblocking the chakras, with specific herbs and specific oils offering different properties for each chakra. Both oils and herbs are used to access information from the spiritual realm and our subconscious and unconscious minds. By using essential oils and essential herbs in our magical practices, we can direct very specific energies towards our intentions for healing, personal growth, and other spells and rituals, of which there are too many to name. They are so powerful that they work outside of our conscious will.

"I hope you enjoy this book as much as I loved writing it. If you do, it would be wonderful if you could take a short minute and leave a review on Amazon as soon as you can, as your kind feedback is much appreciated and so very important. Thank you."

SOURCES

Ezzy, D. (2006). White witches and black magic: Ethics and consumerism in contemporary witchcraft. *Journal of Contemporary Religion 21*(1)15–31. Print.

Greenwood, S. (2015). The anthropology of magic. *Oxford: Berg.* Print.

Magic, Witchcraft and the Otherworld: An Anthropology. *Bloomsbury Academic.* 2000. Print.

Jensen, G. & Thompson, A. (2008). Out of the broom closet: The social ecology of American Wicca. *Journal for the Scientific Study of Religion 47*(4) 753–66. Print.

"magic, n." OED Online, *Oxford University Press,* March 2019

Manning, M. (2014). [Introduction]: Magic, religion, and ritual in historical archaeology. *Historical Archaeology 48*(3)1–9. Print.

Styers, R. (2012). Mana and mystification: Magic and religion at the turn of the twentieth century. *Women's Studies Quarterly 40.*(¾) 226–43. Print.